TO
Julie + Andrew
Happy Cooking
Best Wishes
Peter Easton

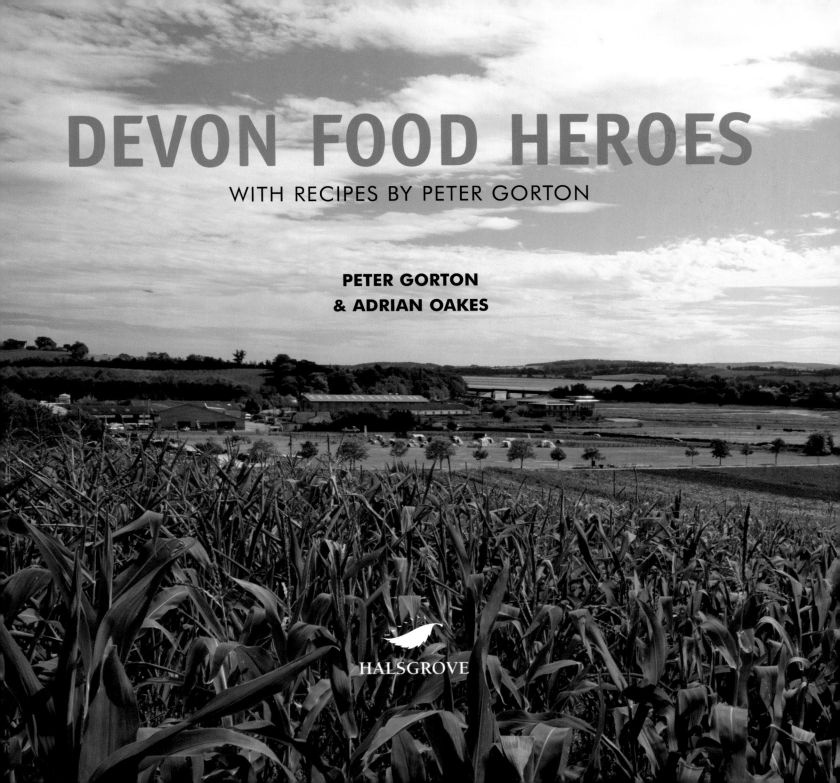

DEVON FOOD HEROES

WITH RECIPES BY PETER GORTON

PETER GORTON
& ADRIAN OAKES

HALSGROVE

Pebblebed Vineyards, Topsham

First published in Great Britain in 2012

Copyright © Images 2012 Adrian Oakes
Copyright © Text 2012 Peter Gorton and Adrian Oakes

Title page photograph: View over Darts Farm near Exeter

British Library Cataloguing-in-Publication Data
A CIP record for this title is available from the British Library

ISBN 978 0 85704 152 4

HALSGROVE
Halsgrove House,
Ryelands Business Park,
Bagley Road, Wellington, Somerset TA21 9PZ
Tel: 01823 653777   Fax: 01823 216796
email: sales@halsgrove.com

Part of the Halsgrove group of companies
Information on all Halsgrove titles is available at: www.halsgrove.com

Printed in China by Everbest Printing Co Ltd

CONTENTS

Bringing in the sheep, Greenwell Farm near Yelverton.

INTRODUCTION

DEVON HAS EXCEPTIONAL food and drink producers and we consider ourselves to be very lucky to have spent time with and written about these truly passionate and remarkable people. Thanks to these gifted people, Devon is fast becoming famous for its award-winning restaurants, food festivals, markets and vineyards. Couple that with Devon's striking coast and wonderful lush countryside the county is truly one to beat. No wonder so many people want to live here.

Many people, myself and Adrian included, are increasingly opting for fresh local produce that hasn't travelled thousands of miles from other countries before reaching our plates. Indeed some of the produce here has travelled less than a mile to the shop. Therefore farm shops and independent artisan producers are becoming more and more important.

The food and drink is not necessarily cheaper but is generally of very high quality. What could be better than enjoying fruit and vegetables that were growing in the field the day before, or meat that has been reared locally and can be traced to the source? Food does not come much better than this.

The producers are also paid a fair price for their goods by supplying smaller individual outlets.

They work in harmony with the retailer which promotes a healthy relationship. All of the producers we spoke to about this had nothing but praise for the people selling their products. After all it's not all about the 'bottom line'. Many of the producers also made a very similar comment 'If we did it just for the money we wouldn't be here'.

Along the way the people we met were enthusiastic about what they do, positive and full of energy. But most importantly of all they were happy with their lot. No dreading the office desk or unscrupulous boss... and no Monday morning feeling. They all said that they had faced varying challenges along the way but their passion for what they do had helped them to find a solution or way forward.

Tourism is an important industry in Devon. The county has numerous attractions encapsulating its natural beauty and without a doubt provides some of the best produce available in Britain today, as we seen have seen for ourselves while gathering information for this book.

We have to say this has been a tremendously exciting and fascinating experience that we will always remember. It has been a true education in the varied and exceptional food and drink available in the county. We have learned about bees, mussels, vegetable growing, preserve making, animal husbandry brewing, viticulture, and ice cream production, amongst many other food-creating activities.

We hope you enjoy this book as much as we enjoyed producing it, and that you will try some of the recipes specially created by Peter to showcase the food and drink producers included here. We each have written various parts of the book and while it may not always be obvious who has written what, the reader can rest assured that we share equally in our enthusiasm for everything we've seen – and consumed!

The people featured in this book are but a small selection of the many high quality producers in Devon. Sadly we couldn't include them all but the list of 'Taste of the West' Devon members at the end of the book gives readers an opportunity to explore the huge variety of foods the county has to offer. We really hope that the producers we met and many others throughout Devon continue to thrive. They certainly deserve to.

They are all out there to be discovered. The true Devon Food Heroes.....

Peter Gorton
Adrian Oakes 2012

A superb ristra from
South Devon Chilli Farm

Fresh and healthy - just some of the produce to be found at Darts Farm

Help pick our sunflowers for

DARTS FARM

History

Darts Farm sits just outside Exeter near Topsham on the edge of a world famous natural bird reserve, the Exe Estuary. The farm was originally run by Ronald Dart with his wife Enid. Over forty years ago Ronald became a pioneer of pick your own and soon started selling vegetables from a shed on the side of the road. I remember 'Pic Fresh', as it was known, from the eighties as I lived nearby and often shopped there. A small greenhouse-like shop with chest freezers and veg displays.

After Ronald died, in 1982, his wife and three sons, Paul, Michael and James progressed the shop, developing farm outbuildings into retail space. Over the last twenty-five years the farm has grown into a truly impressive shopping experience with 20 000 square feet of selling space supporting many local suppliers. Even though the garden shed is long gone, the farm still retains its original feel; the barns are still there though they are now occupied by a varied collection of businesses.

A perfect display of fresh veg.

While Michael and James focus on managing the retail side of the business, Paul Dart manages the 500 acre working farm. Vegetables are grown virtually all year round and Paul rears 100 head of cattle, traditional breeds of course.

Darts Farm has always supported and been loyal to local producers and some have been selling their products at the farm for many decades. I noticed that many of the food producers in this book are sold in Darts Farm's food hall. They support over 200 local businesses and a browse around the food hall is testament to their ethos of high quality local products direct to the customer. The veg looks freshly cut, natural, healthy and distinctly un-processed. Much of the produce is grown on the farm but other varieties are grown locally too.

The food hall has a lovely feel to it, with soft lighting and everything displayed in a pleasant and informal way rather than the regimented 'everything in its place' style of the supermarket. There is a delicatessen which sells over 100 types of cheese, the large veg

section, a top-quality local butcher, the fish shed and a large range of other local produce. There are quirky little corners displaying a varied range of intriguing products and occasional little gems such as cider that is pressed on site, a huge range of bottled ales and chilli sauces produced near Totnes.

Blackboards display information about the suppliers and where the produce comes from and prices that are very competitive considering the quality on display.

Darts Farm is also home to a number of hand picked quality retailers such as Orange Tree, Fired Earth, The Aga Shop, RSPB, Cotswold Outdoor and a florist, as well as their own restaurant and gift, garden, children's clothes and toy departments. A beauty therapist and Pilates studio are located upstairs. They are now offering bike hire at Darts Farm and cyclists can discover the stunning Exe Estuary Cycle Trail, world famous for its birds and beautiful scenery, on a traditional hand-built Pashley bicycle. It's perfectly located between Exeter and Exmouth giving cyclists the opportunity to explore city and sea routes.

When I visited to photograph for the book I spent some time with George, a cheerful, knowledgeable and likeable young character who coordinates all the veg picking and preparation. A very bumpy ride in his old hatchback around the farm led us to the top of the hill with wonderful views across the farm and the Exe Valley behind. Rows of different coloured cabbages and cauliflowers disappeared down the slopes away from us. We walked along rows of onions, runner beans and raspberry canes.

George explained the picking and selection process where only the best is selected for sale in the shop. It is then cut, washed and prepared for sale so the produce is truly fresh and has travelled less then half a mile from the field.

I was actually quite surprised by the range of different vegetables that they grow. This includes squashes, various cauliflowers, cabbages, raspberries, onions, courgettes, potatoes, lots of different green veg and many others types.

A veg cutter working in one of the fields proudly displayed a very healthy looking cabbage. The next 'invasion' was to be pumpkins later in the month.

Back at base we chatted about their longstanding support of local charities. Every year they grow a large field of sunflowers that people are invited to pick. All money raised goes to Hospiscare.

Food Hall at Darts Farm

Supporting local produce

A taste of the growing year on the farm

The cold winter days of January and February, with heavy frosts and a low winter sun can create a beautiful but chilly environment to work in. The Christmas rush is over and the new year has begun.

Some of the cattle that have been fattening through the winter are ready to go to Gerald David's Freedom Food-approved abattoir. All of the meat from the Darts Farm cattle will be sold through Gerald's butchers counter in the farm shop.

The potatoes are being graded ready for the shop and the fields are still yielding staple winter vegetables such as cabbage, sprouts, leeks and kale.

It is also a time of preparation on the farm and there's the healthy country smell of mounds of steaming dung on the fields. Nature's way of fertilising our soil provides us with a bountiful and nutrient-rich ground in which to grow the year's crops.

Autumn is typically an abundant time for the fruits, vegetables and cereals that we grow in the Westcountry and for years our ancestors have marked this by giving thanks with a Harvest Festival.

Harvest Festival is normally held on or near the Sunday of the Harvest Moon. By this time, all the crops have been harvested and the festival is a celebration of the food grown on the land throughout the year. The celebrations in our country date back to pagan times and continue today in churches and schools

During September there is a beautiful field of sunflowers at Darts Farm, the first squashes in all their shapes sizes and colours are ready to eat and Green Valley Cyder are starting their first press of the year.

October is fantastic time on the farm with the fiery autumn sunsets illuminating fields full of intense orange-to-dark-amber pumpkins. It's the perfect time to take a refreshing walk around the fields and see the myriad of autumnal vegetables, from the vibrantly coloured beet leaf to the enormously cumbersome deep-green marrows.

The abundance of vegetables coming out and off of the ground can also be seen at the front of the shop, where Dart Farm's own produce displays are bursting with the seasons offerings. There's beetroot, broccoli, cabbages, cauliflowers, potatoes, celeriac, celery, fennel, kale, brussels sprouts, sweetcorn, apples, quinces, pumpkins, marrows, courgettes and all sorts of varieties of squashes in every shape, size and colour.

In the fields they are busy planting new crops such as spring cabbage, and at the end of the month the wheat will be sewn and the cows brought into the warm for winter store.

DARTS OWN BUNCHED
RHUBARB

£2.49

DARTS OWN BUNCHED
RHUBARB

December can be a very pretty time on the farm. The morning sun twinkles off the frost that covers the ground, and the iced mud crisps under your wellies as you walk around the fields taking in the fresh winter air. At his time of year the fields are bursting with the kinds of vegetables you may see on your Christmas dinner plate, such as sprouts, cabbage and cauliflower, and at Dart's Farm five different types of potatoes are grown. In fact the traditional Christmas lunch is a time when the majority of the country will be dining on possibly the most seasonal produce of the year.

To get ready for the year ahead broad beans, strawberries and oats are now planted. The cattle are fattening up in their sheds away from the icy temperatures. The sheep are

also out in their woolly winter coats maintaining the grass pastures by nibbling away and keeping winter growth under control.

Darts Farm's feel clearly stems back to traditional Devon farming practices and has kept a lot of its unique character which emphasises locally-grown fresh produce, much of it from their own farm which still forms a large part of what they sell. Add in the newer and varied range of retailers and producers included the fantastic Food Hall and you have a great shopping experience that truly showcases the best of Devon.

www.dartsfarm.co.uk

Tartlet case of Darts Farm vegetables on a tomato, ginger and lemongrass-flavoured sauce

Peter Gorton

Tomato, ginger and lemon grass sauce – serves 4

Ingredients
40 x olive oil
10g x garlic finely chopped
40g x red onion, finely chopped
5g x finely chopped ginger
5g x finely chopped lemon grass
6 x large plum tomatoes, skinned and diced
10ml x fish sauce
5ml x lime juice
A pinch of salt and pepper

Method for the sauce
Heat the oil and sauté the garlic, onion, ginger and lemon grass until soft. Add the tomatoes, fish sauce, lime juice and sugar. Simmer for ten minutes, season to taste. Add the chopped coriander leaves just before serving.

Ingredients – serves 4
Homemade or 1 x packet of shortcrust pastry
A selection of Dart's Farm seasonal vegetables
500g x butternut squash, peeled and cut into small dice
250g baby beetroots washed and halved and root removed
2tsp x olive oil
Broccoli florets   (Blanch in boiling water and re-fresh in cold water, set aside and refrigerate)
Cauliflower florets
Fresh garden peas
120g c soft cream cheese
2 x eggs
1 x clove garlic, crushed
Salt and pepper to taste
1 x tablespoon of mixed fresh herbs, chives, basil etc

Method
Pre-heat the oven - 200°C/fan oven 180°C/gas 6/400°F
Place the squash and beetroot on to a baking tray with the oil and toss to coat. Bake in the oven until beginning to colour.

Divide the pastry into six equal portions and roll out to 14cm rounds, press into lightly oiled 12cm round individual tartlet tins, prick the bases with a fork and bake for eight to ten minutes until just beginning to colour.

Wisk together the soft cream cheese, milk, eggs and herbs. Season to taste. Place all the vegetables evenly in the tartlet cases, add the filling and bake for twelve to fifteen minutes until the filling is set.

Assembly
Place a good spoonful of the tomato and ginger, lemon grass-flavoured sauce on the centre of a dinner plate then place the tart on top and serve.

Chef's Tip
I like to serve coriander and basil oils with this dish, it adds a good flavour and makes the dish look attractive.

BASTERFIELD'S HONEY

History

IT WAS WHEN KEN BASTERFIELD was six years old that he was introduced to bees at school, and yet it was some twenty years later that the scent of a beehive brought back those memories.

Overhearing a chance ham radio discussion of how to hive a swarm led to a re-awakening of that latent interest in beekeeping. A quick call got an invitation to join in the activity. Later that summer, and having attended meetings at the Plymouth Beekeepers Association, a barter of radio equipment for a colony of bees led to Ken becoming a beekeeper.

The fascinating world of bees and beekeeping drew Ken in. With a thirst for knowledge, and a realisation steadily dawning of just how much there was to learn, and dissatisfied with the usual folklore and myth, he sought out expert tutoring and mentoring. Classes by the renowned Harrison Ashforth (County Beekeeping Instructor when such posts existed) came first and he began to put some sound science and skills behind the art. Later, being taken under the wing of another great beekeeper, Ken's skills and knowledge grew rapidly.

Bees never do things invariably, the more colonies one sees the more one realises that bees have many ways of coping with life, predators, weather, and problems. The observant beekeeper develops an understanding of, and strategies to cope with, this variability.

Never doing things by halves, a rapid expansion of colony numbers followed, reaching a hundred colonies within eight years.

Life revolved around beekeeping, with wife Maureen and son Daniel involved in all aspects. Conflicts arose, of course: a kitchen sticky with honey doesn't lead to a quiet life! Converting the basement into a honey extracting and bottling room eased matters greatly. Harmony returned, with Maureen looking after produce whilst Daniel, even from a young age, concentrated on managing the bees with his father.

Like any other livestock, bees can be bred for desirable characteristics such as productivity, temperament, health and robustness. Ken would raise new queens to steadily improving the general standard. Now in their 38th year of selection, his bees are healthy, prolific, hard working, frugal, and in demand by other local beekeepers.

Present

Ten years ago a move to East Devon brought the bees to a drier and more productive climate. Daniel in the meantime returned to Devon, seeking a better quality of life and to help expand the family business. Young people bring new visions and plans were laid for centralising all the facilities.

This was to be the first honey farm built in England for nearly twenty years. A modern extracting and bottling room would speed the handling of honey and hive produce, whilst centralised workshops and storage would greatly ease the handling and repair of wooden hive equipment. A classroom, laboratory, and teaching apiary were integral to the plans for the future.

Using a ground source heat pump for heating, and rainwater collection for the water supply, the honey farm has a low carbon footprint and is designed to be part of its environment. Vegetable oil recycled from local pubs and restaurants is converted into biodiesel to power the beekeeping and delivery vehicles. The planned installation of solar PV panels will almost free the honey farm from dependency on outside services, all with a low environmental impact.

The fifty acres of the honey farm are being returned to traditional wildflower meadows. Hedgerows, once regularly flailed, are now being sympathetically managed and allowed to flourish, providing food and safe haven for many birds and small mammals. A large orchard of old Westcountry varieties of apples, pears and plums is being established to further supplement the forage and biodiversity of the site.

Having grown up surrounded by bees and beekeepers Daniel had to hone old skills and refresh old knowledge. Daniel had agreed with his father that he would go through the full British Beekeepers' Association education and examinations system, so that his knowledge would be broad, detailed, and up-to-date. Experiencing the education system as a student encouraged Daniel to start teaching, and to continue studying for the National Diploma in Beekeeping, just as his father had done twenty years before him. The National Diploma is the highest qualification available in beekeeping, and Ken and Daniel Basterfield are the only father and son team to have ever both been awarded it.

Bee heaven in summer

Breeding colony

Honeycombe being spun

Opposite, clockwise from top left:
Smoking the bees; hand
preparation to remove external
wax; filtering the honey; pouring
into jars; modern methods of
production; decanting from a
stainless steel container

The Beekeeping Year

Bees are vegetarians and flowers provide for all their needs. Nectar, stored by the bees as honey, provides the energy source, whilst pollen adds proteins, vitamins, oils and minerals. The natural cycle of the honey bee colony is attuned to the abundance or dearth of flowering plants. Spring brings a period of build up and reproduction (through swarming). Summer is a time of abundance and harvesting; autumn represents preparation for the forthcoming winter. Winter is about survival, waiting for spring and renewal. The stores of honey and pollen that the bees laid in during summer and early autumn will see them through the harshest of winter weather, barring mishaps.

Bee colonies are not domesticated and remain essentially wild, though they do grace us by occupying the hives we provide. They could just as well occupy a chimney or a hollow tree. The role of the beekeeper is not to direct (he couldn't anyway) but to assist the bees in achieving their optimum. Most of the bees still live out on nearby farms pollinating the farm crops and wild flowers alike. They are moved between farms as different crops start and

finish flowering, never great distances but sufficient that they do not confuse their old home with their new one. Bees are excellent navigators, using and remembering landmarks for several miles around, and the wisdom is that you should move a colony "less than three feet, or more than three miles".

In a season, amongst the mixed spring and summer flowering, the bees have their favourites. These include dandelion, oil seed rape, apple & pear, field beans, clover, lime, bramble, and then heather at the end of summer.

In return for their efforts the bees are rewarded with an abundance of honey, and any that is surplus to their needs becomes the beekeeper's reward for his stewardship. The relationship between bees, beekeeper and farmer is one of synergy.

When colonies are moved between farm crops, surplus full honey boxes are removed and empty ones are added. This keeps the hives to a manageable size and weight, and also allows the honey to be harvested in batches through the season.

Honey is still harvested from honeycombs using the traditional processes even in a modern extracting room. The layer of wax sealing the honey is cut away, and then the combs are spun at speed in a simple centrifuge known as an extractor. The honey is thrown from the honeycombs and with it a certain amount of wax and other debris, so it is then lightly filtered to retain all the natural richness of the honey. The filtered honey is left to stand for two days to allow any air bubbles to rise out, before being bottled for sale. The extracting room is kept at a "warm but comfortable" 25°C so that the honey is more fluid.

Future

The new honey farm has been operating for over a year now. The number of colonies is steadily increasing, from its current 140 or so. A local beekeeper has already been employed part-time to help with the management of the bees.

Daniel has great plans for the educational aspect. Having a modern classroom, laboratory, teaching apiary, and honey processing facilities on one site provides training facilities and flexibility unmatched elsewhere in the country. Indeed courses have already been run on behalf of DEFRA, dealing with advanced techniques and bee disease diagnosis. Beekeeping associations from the Westcountry and beyond have come to the honey farm to see the new facilities and equipment, and students from across the country attend the regular courses held there. Whilst he regularly gives lectures around the country, Daniel is keen that people come to Devon, to the honey farm, to experience what it has to offer. Such visitors provide a welcome boost to the local economy.

Remembering their own growing pains, there are plans to make the extracting facilities available to other beekeepers faced with the prospect of having their kitchens taken over by sticky honey processing for a week in the summer. Further supporting local beekeepers, the laboratory facilities will be available for diagnosis of disease and microscopic pests that afflict honey bees.

Whilst he is very much involved in the beekeeping activities, the physical demands of beekeeping mean that Ken is now involved in the areas that do not involve heavy lifting. He won't be put out to pasture just yet though, and he is excited about his plans for the orchard.

Our Visit

During the Summer the authors visited and spent a rewarding afternoon with Ken, Maureen and Daniel learning all about bees.

It was a nice sunny day so I pulled out the convertible and Peter and I headed out. After a wrong turn and an embarrassing fifteen point turn in another farm's courtyard we found Basterfields. A long drive led to a modern collection of buildings set in a large expanse of meadows full of tall grasses and flowers.

We were warmly greeted and shown around the production facility. One large room housed all the equipment necessary to extract and jar the honey. Another room was kept cool for storing the honeycombs before extraction. We were shown a fully set up classroom for beekeeping courses and teaching groups of school children.

After donning protective gear, Ken led us out to the hives. Each one houses approx 60,000 bees and standing near a hive with thousands of bees buzzing around you was an unsettling experience. Adrian managed to get stung even when wearing protective gear from head to foot. Peter just ran away.

Ken told us that they were not aggressive and only react to a threat. 'So don't swat them but ignore them and they will go about their business.' When we were with the hive one thing that stayed with us was the hum of being surrounded by all the bees. We walked around the meadows full of flowers, clover and all sorts of grasses. They encourage a natural habitat around the hives to allow the bees to thrive. Our whole visit, including the family's approach and their understanding of the bees had a lovely feel to it. An excellent example of a food producer really in tune with the whole process from beginning to end.

And the best bit of all is we left with lots of honey!

Cultivating Queen Bees

The authors

shop.the-apiary.com

Basterfield's honey mousse with port jelly and fresh raspberries
Peter Gorton

This is a wonderfully elegant fine dining restaurant dessert, it is simple to make and tastes divine. You can serve it with raspberry sorbet as well if you like.

Method
Bring the milk to simmering point in a saucepan. Whisk the egg yolks and castor sugar in a bowl until pale and frothy, then add the honey and slowly whisk in the warm milk. Stand the bowl over a bain-marie and gently cook, whisking continuously until the mixture coats the back of a spoon.

Soften the gelatine leaves in a little cold water, wring out the excess water and stir the gelatine into the custard until dissolved. Pass the custard through a fine sieve into a clean bowl and cool over ice in the refrigerator. When the custard is almost set (about an hour) fold in the whipped cream and pour into moulds.

To make the jelly - Bring the port and sugar syrup up to the boil in a saucepan. Soften the gelatine leaves in a little water and wring out the excess water and stir the gelatine into the hot liquid until dissolved. Pass the jelly through a fine sieve into a bowl and allow to cool but not set.

To assemble
Spoon the mousse into the desired moulds leaving a gap at the top for the port jelly. Refrigerate until set (about 45 minutes) pour the jelly on top of the mousse. Refrigerate until set (about 1 hour).

To serve
Suspend the moulds in hot water for 30 seconds then carefully turn out on to a shortbread biscuit in the middle of the plate. Place a few raspberries on top of the honey mousse and drizzle a little of Basterfield's wonderful honey over the top. Delicious!

Ingredients – serves 6

Mousse
4 x large eggs yolks
100g x castor sugar
320 ml x milk
60g x honey
2 ½ x gelatine leaves
250 ml x double cream, whipped to stiff peaks

Sugar Syrup
90ml x water
80g x sugar
Boil until dissolved and set aside to cool, refrigerate when cold

Port Jelly
90 ml port
90 x sugar syrup
2 x gelatine leaves

Shortbread biscuits

CRANFIELD'S FOODS

Introduction & History

IT WAS RAINING CATS AND DOGS – but we were not downhearted as we were looking forward to meeting Victoria Cranfield the company owner of Cranfield's Foods – and hopefully to taste her wonderful preserves and pickles. Peter was greeted by George the Rhodesian ridgeback who is the family guardian, and Pickle another Ridgeback who are both bigger than the average dog, and also Toby a cross greyhound. Peter was eaten (only one arm) and I just hovered inconspicuously in the background behind my camera bag. Once we were introduced formally, George became a real sweetie (to Adrian anyway).

Victoria and her beloved George

We were welcomed into the kitchen by Victoria and she told us her interesting story of how she had grown weary of being a lawyer always dealing with other people's problems and thought it was time for a change. Victoria said 'people say much nicer things to me as a cook than a lawyer, and people prefer their tummy's to their problems!

Walking around Victoria's garden, so wonderful and wild and in such a lovely spot nestling in 13 acres on the fringes of Exmoor. There is a wild field neither grazed or mowed or cleared, other than by hand, of brambles. Here are hedgerows bursting with life, so many birds, resident roe deer, toads, frogs and newts, all with their own fascinating eco-systems. Young fruit was appearing under nets and in greenhouses. Adrian took many pictures of the wonderful grounds around the house.

Product

Victoria's homemade jam, marmalade, chutney, condiments and jelly comply to the Slow Food principles, this approach has produced over 50 'Great 'Taste' and 'Taste of the West' awards in their nine years, of which over 14 are Gold. The Grapefruit & Ginger and Blood Orange Marmalades are both stocked by Fortnum & Mason after being well placed in the World Marmalade Awards for two consecutive years. Nearly all of the hand-cut marmalades have won awards.

There is a very special wild pear tree in a private garden in Torrington and is thought to be the only one in Devon. The pears are rock-hard and of little use, seemingly almost made of leather but, offered to her at a local fair, Victoria makes a superb wild pear jelly with them. Victoria trades jars of jelly in return for the fruit.

Victoria has an address book full of people who have quince trees, crab apples and other fruit, happy to trade fruit for preserves. For instance a Macmillan charity supporter in Barnstaple with black and red currants and morello cherries exchanges fruit for preserves to sell in aid of the charity.

Victoria, Louisa and Kate are the three cooks. Louise works out of her own domestic kitchen and has worked with Victoria for six years. Kate helps in Victoria's kitchen. Victoria has a great palate as does her husband Peter and believes in 'taste', that's why her preserves are high in fruit giving a wonderful flavour and with a minimum of fruit content of 60% to 80%, a little will go a long way. With some fruit, she cuts the sugar down to three quarters the weight of the fruit but says she can't go below that because the preserves will not keep – and here's a tip, add a little wine vinegar to the jam to sharpen the flavour and extend the life of the jam.

Victoria told us about the labours of making your own jams. 'It can become very boring,' she says, 'but you can break the process into bite-size chunks. Do a bit one day and the remainder the next' Victoria prepares the fruit in the afternoon, this time with damsons, counting the fruit into the pan and gently stewing in fruit juice. The next day she counts the stones out of the cold mixture wearing thin gloves to avoid stained hands. She then adds the sugar and boils to a set and pours into sterilised jars. She stresses you must count in the stoned fruit so you know how many to take out; no one wants a broken tooth.

Another tip, when making pickles and chutneys, Victoria says always use wine vinegar or cider vinegar, She feels that if you use spirit vinegar you can taste harsh notes on the palate; it will, in her opinion, taint a chutney no matter how good the ingredients are.

Cranfields jellies are boiled to a natural setting point with English sugar balanced with a little wine vinegar. They do not use any artificial pectin's, setting or jelling agents. To have a crystal clear, jewel like jelly from 100% natural ingredients, can only be done if cooked in small batches. This is truly an artisan product and one of her favourites.

Jellies use only the juice of the fruit. Sometimes the juice needs to be liberated by cooking in water but she keeps the water to a minimum to avoid dilution of the flavour. A common base for a flavoured jelly is apple, one with a good natural setting ability. The flower and herb jellies are infused in a bramley apple base.

On the range

Growing tunnel

The hedgerow fruit is picked from her hedges which she manages for natural fruit production. Only taking what they need; the rest is left for the birds and local wildlife. All currants are sourced from within a five mile radius of their kitchen windows, and where possible the herbs are also home grown.

After George had directed us around the garden we retired to Victoria's lovely country kitchen with its Aga and huge central oak table. We spent the afternoon sitting around the table savouring the preserves and chutneys with fresh bread and country cheeses. Victoria presently produces around thirty jellies and over ten chutneys and I think we must have tried most of them. Very little work was done but Adrian did manage some sumptuous shots of the preserves with their constituent fruits and vegetables.

Ready for harvest

Crab Apple and Calvados Jelly

Ingredients
Crab Apples
Water
Sugar
Calvados

Method
Collect and wash your crab apples. Three quarters fill a large saucepan with apples, just cover with water and simmer until soft and disintegrating.

When cooled but still warm (goes through jelly bag quicker) pour through a jelly bag or clean pillow case allow to drip over night. Do not squeeze the bag or the jelly will be cloudy. Measure the resulting liquid. Use in 4 pint batches, 1lb/450g sugar per pint plus quarter pint of wine vinegar.

Bring to a rapid boil in a large saucepan; skim off scum as the jelly come to a boil or it may boil over. Test for a set after 15mins (wrinkle on a saucer) about 219°C Once setting point is reached add a small glass of calvados and decant into sterilized jars.

Damson Jam

Ingredients
2.7kg (6lb) damsons
2kg (4.5lbs) sugar
290ml (0.5pint) orange juice
Zest 1 orange

Method
Count the washed fruit into a saucepan (tells you how many stones need to come out)

Add the zest and juice of orange and simmer until soft. Let go cold and with clean hands/plastic gloves count out all stones.

Warm fruit and add sugar, bring to a boil stirring until the sugar has dissolved.
Rapid boil for 10mins (occasionally stir to check not sticking) test for set (wrinkle on saucer)
Pour into sterilized jars. Makes approximately 9lbs

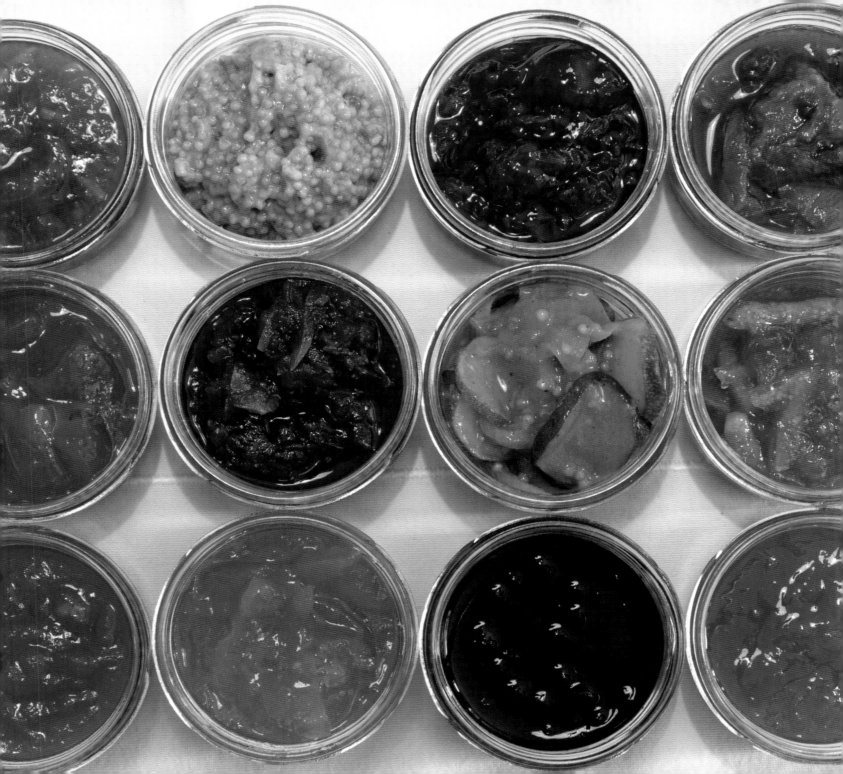

Victoria works in collaboration with local fruit growers to ensure good supplies of local fruit and   makes preserves for Arlington Court, the local National Trust property. Fruit trees and bushes have been planted to cut down food miles and there is a strong environmental ethos reusing, recycling and composting, Victoria does not use pesticides or herbicides, letting nature take its course and share fruit with the birds. The produce from Arlington Court's walled garden is picked in the morning and cooked the same day with British sugar, total food miles........one.

About a 1,000 jars go to Arlington, Victoria buys the fruit from the walled garden and using the fruit produces as many jars for resale by Arlington as they order, the rest goes into her own products,   All their black and red currants, strawberries, tayberries, onions, courgettes, pears and the list goes on depending on the season.

Another tip, Victoria always freezes rhubarb even if she is using it the next day, she says if you freeze the fruit which has a high water content it will give off half the liquid as it thaws cutting cooking time.

Chocolates are Victoria's latest baby, we recommend 'Truffles with Attitude' for their award winning, made to order, fresh cream double centred truffles. Each truffle contains Cranfields jelly with a complimentary flavoured chocolate ganache.

The Calvados Truffles were awarded Gold ** and the Sloe Gin Truffles Gold * at the Great Taste Awards this year. In addition 4 bronze awards were given by the Taste of the West. Still an embryonic Company in its own right and lacking its own website at present, truffles can be ordered through her for Weddings and corporate gifts. Flavour is literally at the centre of each truffle.

The future for Victoria? She says she wants to stay small and stay with small independents, it's manageable and won't sell out to the big boys and one day she plans to write a book so anyone can follow her recipes. She has learnt a lot as we have. We thanked Victoria for a lovely lunch and the chance to taste her wonderful preserves and pickles.

We waved her and the dogs goodbye and headed down the drive. I am sure we will return again.

www.cranfieldsfoods.co.uk

Wonderful truffles

Roasted pork tenderloin on creamy garlic and rosemary polenta and Victoria Cranfield's soused cherries
Peter Gorton

Ingredients – Serves 6
2 x trimmed pork tenderloins
Olive oil
1 x jar Cranfields Soused English Cherries

Roast Garlic
3 x heads garlic
1 x tablespoon olive oil
Salt & pepper
1 x sprig thyme
1 x sprig rosemary

Polenta
700ml x full cream milk
150ml x double cream
2 x sprigs rosemary
110g x polenta (yellow cornmeal)
50g x Parmesan cheese, freshly grated
1 tablespoon unsalted butter
Salt & pepper
6 x cloves of roasted garlic, as above

Method
Pre-heat oven to 220°C/fan oven 200°C/gas 7

Heat a large frying pan with the olive oil and seal the pork all over until golden brown. Remove from the pan and transfer to a baking tray, season with salt and pepper and bake for 12 minutes, take out and rest for ten minutes before serving.

CREAMY GARLIC AND ROSEMARY POLENTA

Roast Garlic
Method
Cut the garlic in two across the head to expose the cloves. Drizzle the oil, season and set cut down on the herbs on an oiled oven tray. **Bake for 1 hour at 120°F/fan oven 100°C/250°F/gas ½**

Polenta – (this is a generous amount!)
Method
Place milk, cream, rosemary and garlic in a saucepan and bring almost to a boil. Pour the polenta into the milk and whisk well until blended. Stir constantly over moderate heat until mixture returns to the boil. Reduce the heat to low and cook stirring often for about 20 minutes or until the polenta is cooked and thickened. Fold in the Parmesan cheese and butter, season to taste.

To Assemble
Put one or two tablespoons of polenta in the centre of six warm dinner plates. Carve the pork fillet into equal slices, each pork tenderloin will serve three people. Arrange the pork on the polenta and surround with Victoria's wonderful cherries, accompany with vegetables of your choice and a red wine sauce.

Chefs Tip
Cranfields Soused English cherries in sweet vinegar syrup will accompany duck and will also make a wonderful addition to a casserole.

Cranfields
Soused English Cherries
For game or beef

DARTMOOR BREWERY

History

DARTMOOR BREWERY is based in Princetown high up on the moor, not far from the prison. This is the home of the famous Jail Ale. Dartmoor brewery claims to be the highest in England at 1400 feet above sea level.

The brewery was started by Simon Loveless, a former Gibbs Mew & Hopback brewer, who started brewing in 1994 in a converted garage behind the Prince of Wales pub in the centre of Princetown. It was soon realised there was a great demand for high quality real ale so over the years the company has expanded.

Production increased to 60 barrels a week by 1998, supplying four pubs owned by a sister company and about 40 local pubs direct. A further expansion occurred in 2005 when £1 million was invested in a new German-built plant behind the old premises with support from Dartmoor National Park and the Duchy. The new brew-length is 33 barrels with the ability to produce 66 barrels a day five days a week. The original company, Princetown Brewery, was renamed Dartmoor Brewery in May 2008.

I spent a day with the Master Brewer Mike Lunney who joined the brewery two years ago after a long career in brewing, first with Whitbread and then Gale's of Horndean. A fascinating day it was too.

I walked around the brewery looking up at huge stainless steel fermentation vessels, pipes and tanks, with panels blinking with lights and gauges. At one end casks were being steam-cleaned for sterilisation before being filled with ale. Spotlessly clean bottles, ready for filling and labelling, sat in another corner. Upstairs is where the bottling happens, all still by hand. Their brightly signwritten vans come and go delivering to various pubs and shops in the area.

After a chat and cup of tea we moved deeper into the details of the brewery production methods. Mike explained the brewing process as I watched him empty malt sacks into the crusher, the grist for the mill.

Perfect ingredients make the perfect pint.

Cleaning Casks

The brewing process consists of malting of the barley, mashing, boiling, fermentation, racking, conditioning and finally, the best stage, drinking.

The premium malting barley is produced by Tucker's of Newton Abbot. Malting involves soaking the grain and allowing it to germinate over 3 days. It is then dried and kilned for delivery to the brewer.

The malt is sent through a crusher and then mixed with hot water to get to 65°C and left for an hour. This produces a pale sweet solution called wort. This is then moved to a boiling vessel called the copper or wort kettle. These were all modern-looking vessels made of stainless steel. The brewer regularly checked various stages, opening hatches and watching gauges. Mike opened a lid on a vessel and gestured for me to have a look. The mash was mixing before moving onto the boiling stage.

Hops are added to the sweet wort mixture and the whole thing is boiled for one and a half hours. More hops are added at the end of the boil. An inspection window was opened resulting in a plume of steam as the mix boiled.

This hopped wort is then transferred to a whirlpool hop separation vessel before cooling to 15 degrees C as it is pumped to the huge fermentation vessels.

Opposite, clockwise from top left: Adding ingredients; the head brewer keeping an eye on things; bottling; capping bottles; casks ready for filling

Sampling from the fermentation vat

The Dartmoor Brewery gang

The brewer showed me the inside of a huge fermentation vessel through a small hatch. The yeast was sitting at the bottom waiting for the wort to be added. This temperature controlled process takes 4 days followed by a cooling and resting stage of 2-4 days. The resulting liquid is known as green beer and is transferred to a racking tank and is then pumped into casks with finings to clear the beer of yeast.

With real ale the cask conditioning process allows further fermentation as the yeast continues to work on the sugar that is left in the beer, maturing and developing the flavour. Most of the beer is racked into casks for delivery to pubs, but a small percentage goes for bottling as bottle conditioned beer.

Dartmoor Brewery produce a range of delicious beers, all of which we have sampled. From the famous and our personal favourite, Jail Ale, to Legend, Dartmoor IPA, Friggins, Dragons Breath and Three Hares ale, the last made with Dartmoor heather honey.

Friggins was launched early in 2011 to help expansion into Cornwall. Guests at the Jamaica Inn on Bodmin Moor were among the first to taste Dartmoor Brewery's latest beer as the first pints of Friggins were served up at a special launch event there.

The pirate-themed launch was timed to coincide with the release of the fourth film instalment of *Pirates of the Caribbean*, the four per cent ale is targeting local real ale fans as well as visitors.

Brewer Mike Lunney believes the new beer will help build up their presence in the Cornish market. "We wanted to maintain the balance of our portfolio of beers with an exciting new brew that both complements our existing products and appeals to a new drinkers."

Made using traditional brewing techniques and a unique hop blend, Friggins is a highly drinkable thirst-quenching beer with delicious lemon and slightly spicy fruit flavours on the aftertaste.

Jail Ale is a full-bodied mid brown beer with a well rounded flavour and a sweet moorish aftertaste. This is the brewery's best known ale.

Dartmoor IPA is a highly drinkable, amber coloured beer and has a delicious thirst-quenching taste with a subtle hop aroma.

The well-established Dartmoor Legend ale has a combination of cool pure Dartmoor water, the finest Devon grown malted barley and the best English hops, creating a classic cask-conditioned beer. Smooth, full of flavour and balanced with a delicious crispy malt fruit finish.

Peter selected Dartmoor Legend as being ideal for the recipe he created for the book: braised beef in Dartmoor Legend Ale with creamy garlic and rosemary polenta.

Dartmoor brewery has won a host of awards for its beer. These include many gold awards from SIBA South West malting Beer festival, and Champion at the South Devon Camra Beer Festival, Plymouth Beer Festival and the Cotswold Beer Festival, amongst many others.

We were impressed and fascinated by the brewery and the friendly atmosphere whilst visiting the business. They have a wonderful range of pure Devon products and we are sure that they will flourish in the years to come and no doubt other ales will arrive in the future. We would recommend that you try their ales, you will be smitten. We also invite you to try the following recipe using their beer – it's delicious.

www.dartmoorbrewery.co.uk

Dartmoor Brewery beef stew with creamy mashed potatoes

Peter Gorton

This is a classic recipe made with Dartmoor Legend ale. I feel it adds a lovely flavour and with the creamy mash potatoes it's a marriage made in heaven!

Method
Pre-heat the oven- fan 140°C fan oven/gas 2

Coat the diced meat in the two tablespoons of flour, heat the olive oil in a casserole dish, when it is hot add the meat in small batches, brown evenly and set aside.

Turn the heat down and add the roughly chopped onions, cook until turning brown then add the chopped celery, carrots and garlic and cook for a further two minutes.

Now add the meat back to the casserole dish heat through for two minutes then add the passata, Legend Ale, soy sauce or Worcestershire sauce, mustard, two sprigs of thyme and the three bay leaves. Bring to a simmer. Place a tight fitting lid on the casserole and cook in a low oven until cooked, about three hours. The meat should be very tender.

Potato Purée – Method

Peel the potatoes before cooking. Drop the potatoes into cold salted water, bring to the boil and cook until soft. If you are using new potatoes cook them in their skins to avoid an elastic texture otherwise. Purée them through a rice press or a hand masher.

Add cold butter, mix then adjust the seasoning, just before serving gradually add warm cream or milk until you achieve the right consistency.

Ingredients – serves 6

1 kg stewing steak – cut into pieces
3 x onions/ chopped
3 x sticks of celery/chopped
3 x carrots/ chopped
4 x cloves Garlic
2 x sprigs of thyme
3 x bay leaves
Olive oil
2 x heaped tablespoons of flour
500ml x Dartmoor Legend Ale
200ml X passata (sieved tomatoes)
1 x tablespoon soy sauce or Worcestershire sauce
2 x tablespoons of Dijon mustard

Potato Purée

800g x Maris Piper potatoes
100g x butter
100ml x milk, warmed
Salt and Pepper
Add cream to taste

PEBBLEBED WINES

History

GEOFF AND ANNA BOWEN own and run Pebblebed Vineyards in a wonderful part of Devon near Topsham.

'It all started as a bit of fun' says Geoff. 'A community project amongst friends.' Geoff set the project up in an adjacent field owned by friends Gail and David Leeder. The half acre orchard near Ebford was named after the house 'Eden'. Local families were invited to get involved and learnt to tend the vines, harvest and benefit from sharing the wine.

Geoff, originally an Environmental Geologist, soon realised he had a real passion for viticulture and in 2002 planted the Ebford main field. This was the start of the commercial Pebblebed vineyards. If you look left when travelling out of Clyst St George towards Woodbury you will see the vineyard stretching up the hillside. They now have 20 acres of vines that produce virtually all their grapes. He is proud of the fact that all their grapes come from the Exe Valley, a small percentage to support their main crop coming from a few local growers.

Juliet and Roger White at Yearlstone Vineyard who became great friends over time are expert wine producers with many years of experience. They

Ann and Geoff

Grapes going into the vat

Picked grapes

presently produce the wine for Geoff and store it in his new vats on their premises, allowing Geoff to gain experience and build the business whilst still producing a good volume of excellent wine per year. I visited Yearlstone with Geoff to experience the grape pressing and met Juliet and Roger. Geoff speaks very fondly of them and intends to keep their 'wine relationship' strong in the future.

Geoff is married to Anna and has two young children, Martha and Jessie. He sold his successful Environmental Consultancy business in 2004 to focus totally on Pebblebed, although he is still a Trustee with the Devon Wildlife Trust.

Geoff immediately struck me as an energetic and charismatic character and is obviously very well liked by all around him. He has a very strong team ethic and actively encourages people to 'get involved at any level.' He humorously added 'I don't say get off my land! But come and join me.' A very refreshing and admirable ideal.

The family also have a charming wine cellar in Topsham from where they invite people to come and socialise, eat and enjoy their wines. Vineyard tours and are offered during the summer and wine tasting sessions are regularly enjoyed by many.

Picking goes on whatever
the weather

The Product
Pebblebed has vineyards on two nearby sites at Ebford and Clyst St George just to the south of Exeter. You can find out more about their wines by visiting their excellent website.

The Vineyards
EBFORD. Following the successful planting of the Ebford Eden Community Vineyard, the Ebford Vineyard Main Field was planted in 2002 with 2 acres of Seyval Blanc, 0.5 acres of Madeleine Angevine and 0.5 acres of Rondo on land leased from Dr and Mrs Leeder. In 2005 a further 5 acres was planted with Pinot Noir Early along the Ebford slope in both directions. Planting of the vines was a grand affair with Club Vino members, friends and locals assisting. Local farmers John and Jane Pyne have given considerable assistance and support in the establishment of the vineyard.

CLYST ST GEORGE This vineyard is on the next ridge of hills about 1km to the north of the Ebford Vineyard on land owned by John and Jane Pyne. The geology and aspect is similar, sloping gently to the south underlain by sandy marl deposits of the Exmouth Formation.

A helping hand

The Harvest
Our visit was at the busiest time during the full-on grape harvest. Local people turn up with their children in large numbers enthusiastically brandishing a pair of snips and ready to work. Geoff chatted about the friends and supporters as he set up the refreshments in their wonderful old French delivery van that can often be seen parked in the Clyst St George vineyard entrance. A great community feeling was evident even though it is now a commercial operation.

The day started with grey skies and drizzle but the people came, chatting and laughing in wellies and raincoats ready and willing. Later in the morning we were blessed with blue skies with warm sunshine sun and the picking soon produced huge stacks of brimming crates.

I chatted to people as I wandered taking photographs and the prevailing response was 'we do this because we enjoy it'. A cheerful young boy in a bright red raincoat giggled as he loaded his little wheelbarrow with red grapes. I chatted to his parents and really felt that I was standing in the centre of a great project with real community spirit. But a strong project needs to be guided by drive and enthusiasm which is provided by Geoff.

A number of the rows of vines have name tags. People can invest in these in return for wine every year. I wandered to the top of the slopes and enjoyed the wonderful views over the vineyard towards the Exe Valley.

After a long day the crates of grapes were loaded by Geoff with a little 'help' from yours truly into a large trailer and hitched to his green Land Rover. They didn't all fit! Geoff immediately thought of a plan B and a second trip was organised for the rest. Never did his enthusiasm waver even when he was wondering how many pickers would arrive earlier in the day when the rain hindered things.

We then headed off to Yearlstone Vineyard to see Juliet and Roger. Throughout the whole day, even when the heavens opened as people arrived to pick, Geoff's enthusiasm never wavered.

A short journey over to Bickleigh brought us to Yearlstone and after a brief discussion as to the plan of action, Roger and Geoff started the process of unloading the grapes for pressing. An interesting looking contraption with a large funnel protruding from the top crushes the grapes, pumps the juice into large stainless steel vats and pushes all the remaining stalks and skins out of an opening at the end. The whole process took very little time. The juice is then ready for its slow journey to the bottle. Large fermenting vats are cleaned and ready for the wine fermentation. These are owned by Geoff and will eventually be located at Geoff's own winery that is planned for construction.

Tasting at the cellars

The Future

Geoff and Anna recently bought Marianne Pool Farm including all the land that the Clyst St George vines inhabit. The land available allows the expansion of the vineyards in the future. They feel fortunate to have been able to acquire land that is literally next door to the Clyst St George Vineyard – this has allowed the planting of their new 'Dragons Den' partner vineyard and will allow a new winery to be prepared, hopefully for the 2012 vintage.

The new partner vineyard came about as a result of the BBC Dragons Den programme where Geoff pitched an idea to plant a new vineyard where new people can join in and have the same experiences he has had over the last ten years in setting up, nurturing, harvesting and eventually drinking the wine produced. Geoff entered the Den and just about came out alive with the backing of Dragon Duncan Bannatyne. About thirty individuals, businesses, and educational organisations have joined the project and it is hoped more people and businesses will join in future plantings.

The iconic French van

The view over Eden

Geoff says, "We have planted resistant vines which will require very little spraying with chemicals – looking ahead this is the future for viticulture and agriculture as a whole. We will look to make sparkling wine with our trusted Seyval and Rondo grapes and look for some interesting red wines, blending Regent with Rondo and Pinot Noir. Solaris will be used for blending with our Seyval for still whites and possibly to make a dessert wine."

Geoff and Ann have very defined ideas on how they would like Pebblebed to grow and are very enthusiastic about the future of Devon wines as an industry. I am sure that the quality of the wine will be paramount in their plans as their hearts are definitely in the business. Its not just a job but a way of life that effects them in many ways. With a host of awards I am sure we will enjoy their wines for may years to come.

www.pebblebed.co.uk

Roasted partridge with braised red cabbage and Pebblebed red wine poached pears

Peter Gorton

Ingredients – serves 4

4 x young partridges about 255g each in weight
2 x teaspoons unsalted butter
2 x teaspoons grape seed oil
Salt and ground white pepper
2 x rashers or smoked bacon

Method

In a large frying pan heat the butter and oil and brown the partridges for 2 minutes on each thigh and 30 seconds on each breast. Turn them on their backs and place half a rasher of smoked bacon on top of each partridge and roast for 12 minutes. Pour off the fat and leave to rest for a few minutes in a warm place, covered with greaseproof paper.

Braised Red Cabbage

Method
Remove and discard any outer damaged leaves, cut into quarters and cut away the hard cores, thinly shred the cabbage.

Put the olive oil in a large pan, heat and add sliced cabbage and stir for 10 minutes until all the cabbage is coated, add the grated apple, sliced onions and redcurrant jelly, cook for 10 minutes. Add the red wine, reduce the heat and slowly cook for 45 minutes stirring occasionally. The liquid should have evaporated. Set aside.

Chefs Tip
If you want to prevent your red cabbage 'bleeding' over your plate and into your sauce, ten minutes before the cabbage is cooked add a grated potato.

Red Wine and Rosemary Poached Pears

Method
In a medium saucepan boil all the ingredients for two minutes. Add the pears, simmer for about ten minutes. Remove the pan from the heat and let the pears sit for about fifteen minutes. Keep the pears in their liquid until cold then refrigerate. When ready to serve slice the pears and either place under the grill or in the oven to warm to warm through.

To Assemble
Place the hot red cabbage on the centre of four pre-heated plates, carve the partridge and place on the cabbage, place the pears on the plate beside the partridge and serve immediately

Ingredients
Braised Red Cabbage
1 x red cabbage
Olive oil
1 x Apple grated
1 x tablespoon of redcurrant jelly
Red wine
Pebble Bed red wine

Red Wine and Rosemary Poached Pears
4 x peas, peeled, halved lengthwise and cored
600ml water
150g sugar
600ml Pebble Bed red wine
1 x large sprig Rosemary
1 x cinnamon stick (optional)

Barney with the press

SANDFORD ORCHARDS

History

WE FIRST MET BARNY in the spring for a chat about our book and talked about the history of the orchard, all about the apples and where he wants to be in the future. "I am an Apple bore," he admitted with grin. I find that most people that are passionate about something they do well are often the same. We knew he was one for our book.

Barny grew up in the parish of Sandford in Crediton where the 'cidery' is now based. A love affair with the apple tree stems back to when he was just big enough to climb one. Scrumping for apples was one of his favourite pastimes. After a spell at university Barny returned to Sandford and started making cider in 2003. "I wasn't on a good enough salary to buy the amount of cider a young man needs, so I had earn more or make my own!" Barny's passion for the apple blossomed (pardon the pun) and the cider business grew. "I have worked on farms for many years and I think you become hooked on the life." Barny knew that local farmers who had known him for years would let him have some apples. "I took them to a local cider maker and had them pressed."

Sandford Orchards as a commercial enterprise was set up by Barny Butterfield in 2003 and they got their own press in 2004. The land around Crediton is very good for apples as it drains well and has the right Ph. Given a chance, Barny will bore you about soil too!

He lives on the farm with his wife Marie and their two sons Alfie and Elliott. The farm is presently rented from the local council as an incentive and support to new enterprise. There is no doubt this has helped Barny to kick things off and encourages expansion, enabling Sandford Orchards to move to a more permanent location in the future.

The holding comprises a small red brick farmhouse and selection of very old barns and newer, larger outbuildings. One of the barns with the most character is used to display the various bottles and casks sitting on top of what looks like equally aged barrels. The newer buildings house a selection of giant wooden cider vessels and another houses the bottling plant. Wooden crates full of apples sit around waiting for their 'big squeeze'. This is where

The old barn

The farm

the main commercial production happens. Barny showed us round and pointed out the well-used hand-operated hydraulic cider press. "We are hoping to get a belt press soon," Barny says. "To speed things up a bit."

A giant blackboard sits on one wall with prices and other details all over it. Pallets of packed cider are stored everywhere in the main buildings. The scale of the business was larger than I originally expected when arriving and all seems to be run in a relaxed but efficient manner by Barny. His cheerful, enthusiastic and positive nature exuded as we walked around, commenting about the cider, apples and the challenges that were regularly accompanied by a chuckle. Things aren't always plain sailing but the challenges in life make you stronger. I got a strong impression that Barny would overcome pretty much any obstacle thrown at him during his cider journey

Barny pointed out some huge wooden cider vats in one of the main buildings. "I will climb on to one of them for a photo if you like." Next thing we were clambering around and scaling ladders to check out a vantage point, Barny balanced on top of the vats whilst I set up the flash guns to take the shot looking up through the gap between them. He smiled and held up a glass of his finest for the shot. I suspect his adventurous nature stems back to scrumping for apples as a lad.

The main visit was during apple heaven (mid October). Barny has always been keen to keep the traditional skills alive alongside the profitable more modern processes, and once a year he presses apples at Prowse Farm with the Stoyle family, who have been making cider there for well over a hundred years. He has a modern bottling plant back at base and all the equipment to produce quality cider in large enough quantities to supply all his customers and retailers, but the traditional cider press sounded wonderful for the book.

I have a real fascination for old farms with their interesting collections of oak beamed barns and outbuildings and this one ticked all the boxes. A wonderful old farmhouse with a gorgeous black Labrador, Jack, who wandered over barking and then immediately palled up with me as I disembarked to look for the 'gang'.

I heard voices so investigated with Jack alongside to help. I walked around a corner to find Barny, his sister, the farmer and friends standing in a very old barn looking at an ancient hand-hewn wooden cider press comprising large wooden base from which rose a massive threaded iron shaft.

The process which takes most of a day consists breaking down the apples to allow them to be pressed for their juice and gradually building up repeating layers of reed, straw and apple pulp on the wooden base of the press.

Once a year the old cider press is used

Firstly the apples were loaded through a hole in the barn wall into a pulping machine hidden in the bowels of the farm floor. This was powered by an old tractor and a canvas belt. The tractor looked similarly aged but ticked away without a hint of a problem until the apples were all ready for the press. Then its 'all hands on deck'. The layers are gradually built up and packed around the central iron shaft in a pyramid fashion. The press will hold two tons when ready for the pressing.

Next comes a large wooden plate topped off by a huge lever with an iron ratchet. Into this is placed a big wooden bar that looked suspiciously like a tree branch. Then two people start winding the plate down the threaded shaft by repeatedly turning the bar, backing off as the iron rachet clicked backwards for the next pass. Eventually, as the pressure on the apples increases, the juice starts to flow quite quickly into a wooden barrel. This is then pumped into larger sealed wooden barrels. After many turns the pressure becomes so great that two can no longer push the bar, so more and larger people are added. At last another vertical bar is strapped between the floor and ceiling of the barn and a rope lashed to the end of the main bar to add 'leverage' and exert even more pressure on the apples. The large wooden beams of the press flex under the pressure but at no time did I feel they would give way. After all this press has been used for many decades. I was amazed at the sheer volume of juice that was squeezed from the apples.

It was fascinating and enjoyable to watch this ancient cider making process still being used and my hat goes off to Barny and the gang for keeping this skill alive. After the pressing, when the juice was safely stored in the wooden barrels, we sat in the orchard and enjoyed an impromptu barbeque of his home-produced bacon and chatted about you guessed it… cider!

The more commercial side of the business seems to be buoyant and is growing. Barny is enthusiastic about the future, with new retailers on the books and an increase in production planned. A major national retailer has asked Sandford Orchards to produce a special cider for them which is due to hit the shelves early in 2012.

Eventually he will leave the farm for more permanent premises and I am sure Sandford Orchards cider will be found in many more corners of the UK. Barny has plans for increased production on a larger scale but I doubt he will ever forget the early days scrumping for apples.

The many awards received by Sandford Orchards are testament to the quality of the cider they produce, and having sampled most of his variations I heartily agree.

www.sandfordorchards.co.uk

Barney on top of the world

Ginger Sponge Pudding with Caramelised Apples and Caramel Sauce

Peter Gorton

I love ginger sponge pudding, it's one of my personal favourites!

Cake Preparation – Pre-heat oven to 180°C/fan oven 160°C/gas 4

Cream the butter and sugar until light, beat in the eggs and fold in the cream and the vanilla essence. Sift the flour, bi-carb and spices and carefully fold into the mixture.

Grease 6 metal pudding moulds and place them on a baking tray, fill the moulds and bake in the oven for about 20 minutes or until they spring back to the touch.

Apple and caramel sauce – Method

Put the sugar into a frying pan over a medium heat and cook the sugar until it is golden brown, add the apples and caramelise with the sugar until apples are golden brown. Add the Sandford Orchard Cider and reduce it by a half then add the, butter, vanilla bean pulp, and cream and cook until you have a nice caramel sauce. Set the sauce aside until ready to pour over the puddings.

Warm the cakes in the oven for a few moments, set at 150°C/fan oven 130°C/gas 2.

Place the puddings on dessert plates then put the caramelised apples on top and pour over the caramel sauce. Serve with vanilla ice-cream or clotted cream.

Ingredients

Ginger Sponge Pudding

100g x butter
125g x soft brown sugar
2 x eggs
125ml/double cream
1 x teaspoon vanilla essence
125g x plain flour
1 x teaspoon bi-carbonate of soda
1 x teaspoon ground cinnamon
2 x teaspoons ground ginger

Apple and caramel sauce

280g x sugar
55g x unsalted butter
225ml x double cream
225ml Sandford Orchard
3 x peeled, cored and each apple cut into 8 segments
Pulp of a ½ vanilla bean (optional)

Mat and his father Arnold at Greenwell

DARTMOOR FARMERS
'Real Beef and lamb'

History

DEEP WOODED GORGES, tumbling rocky rivers, winding stonewalls – welcome to Dartmoor National Park and the setting for some of the country's finest reared beef and lamb. Adrian was particularly relaxed as this is almost his second home, having three of his photography books published about the moor.

More than 6,000 years of settled agriculture has created Dartmoor's unique upland landscape and environment today, livestock grazing is seen as one of the most important factors in preserving the very special qualities of Dartmoor's moorland.

Back in 2007 a group of Dartmoor Hill farmers formed the Dartmoor Farmers' Association with the support of HRH The Prince of Wales. The idea was to support farming on the moor and to produce the best in British meat.

Dartmoor is known as one of the most distinctive and beautiful of Britain's National Parks and is a true wilderness in parts. Livestock have grazed the open moor for many hundreds of years, feeding on uncultivated grasslands. This ensures the ecology of the moor remains largely unchanged. The ethos of the Association is summed up as follows:

"Our passion, both for the beauty of Dartmoor and a belief in the importance of farming native breeds of sheep and cattle in this unique landscape in an environmentally sensitive way, is the underlying principle behind our organisation. We believe that expert husbandry, honed over generations, and using to our advantage the landscapes of Dartmoor National Park provides unique beef and lamb of exceptional quality and flavour."

The combination of natural grazing and traditional methods have resulted in some of the best livestock produced anywhere, winning Dartmoor Farmers many awards for the quality and taste of their meat.

The Association comprises thirty hill farms spread around the moor producing quality

Display at butchers

Flock of sheep with Dartmoor in the background

lamb and beef. They champion a first-class product with no compromise, and try to move away from the commodity-driven supply towards a premium meat brand. The key to this is to work in harmony with the beautiful moorland landscape, maintaining the environment for its wildlife, recreation and tourism.

Greenwell Farm

One of our planned visits for this book was to one of the many excellent farms within the Dartmoor Farmers Association.

Greenwell Farm sits on the edge of Dartmoor near Yelverton. Arnold, a long standing Dartmoor farmer with a likeable, interesting character and a strong Devon accent told me about the farm and its history. They produce beef and lamb, the cattle being mainly Galloway and South Devon breeds. He runs the farm with the help of his two sons Neil and Mat. Mat arrived soon after in their short wheel base Land Rover. A plan of action was discussed and we hopped in the Land Rover and headed off.

Matthew Cole is one of the Dartmoor farmers whose family have farmed here for three generations. He knows very well that only the toughest native breeds of sheep and cattle can survive on the moor. For example when there is snow and ice you will see modern commercial breeds of sheep just standing there and looking miserable while their own native sheep dig through the snow and eat the heather tips and other small shrubs which they love. They are perfectly adapted to life up in this harsh environment. They keep two breeds, Whiteface Dartmoors and Scotch Blackface. Mat told Adrian how vital it is for the moor that they do so; without grazing the rare habitats will disappear and access to walkers would be impassable. Adrian said that he has often used livestock tracks on the open moor to guide him through boggy areas.

Mat at Greenwell Farm

The cattle spend the summer on the moor and return to the farm in autumn. They actually prefer being out on the moor and this in part adds to the quality of the meat.

"We like to breed Pedigree Galloway's as they make great mothers and breed very well. Due to the rough herbage they feed on when out on the moor. With no fertilisation or cultivation they grow more slowly which in turn creates meat with an improved flavour, a meat which becomes marbled with fat which makes it extra juicy when cooked," says Mat. They also breed South Devon cattle that are more suited to the better land in the valleys.

Arnold says that when the cattle are out on the open moor they are difficult to move as they know this is home to them. Livestock have grazed the open moor this way for hundreds of years which helps to preserve the natural environment and keeps the traditional methods

Contented livestock

alive. The Dartmoor Farmers' Association many awards are testament to this traditional way of livestock farming.

I was given a tour of a small part of the considerable area covered by the farm, with extensive views of the moor from almost every spot.

From a very noisy herd of South Devon's to large flocks of sheep we headed practically as the crow flies across the fields. I asked Mat why the cows were making so much noise. He told me that they think they are moving to a new field with fresh grazing, but such movement is carefully controlled so the animals don't over eat and they are periodically moved from field to field only when they need it.

The cows looked fantastically healthy and the environment where they are bred is testament to this. Very hilly, lots of fresh air, natural grazing and no artificial ingredients at all!

We then came across a large flock of sheep. Mat attracted them over for a photo with a large bag of feed. A very lively young Collie finished the round up. These sheep also graze out on and roam the moor within certain areas on the commons. They are identified to particular farms by coloured markings.

The livestock is brought in from the open moor in autumn within the protection and security of the farm during the winter months which can be extremely harsh on the high moorland. Having them close to the farm also makes it easier to feed them.

Back at the farm Mat brought a ram out of a horse box. I was taken aback by the size of him (and his horns!). He was very lively with piercing, wide eyes and looked a picture of health. Matt's Father, Arnold, arrived back in their new tractor and we had a short chat about the farm as they posed with the tractor for a photo. "Lets get down the pub," Arnold proclaimed in his broad Devon accent. Work was done, for a little while anyway.

When Mat and a number of other farmers decided to work together to sell their meat under the label Dartmoor Farmers' Association, it was an initiative in part due to the inspiration and backing of Prince Charles. Their brand logo is that of an iconic moorland clapper bridge taken from a painting by the Prince and denoting to the Association a reminder of the Dartmoor landscape.

Five years on, the Association now supplies meat from a guaranteed native breed and entirely raised on the moor. The project has been a great success, with good sales locally and now buyers and chefs in London are also keen to try this wonderful produce. The meat from the moor scooped the best of meat and poultry award for 2010 'Taste of the West', and in 2011 'The Carol Trewin South West Producer of the Year' award. Their produce has also won three individual gold awards for their rack of lamb, ribs of beef and lamb steaks.

Mat with the ram

Mat with livestock

A Lyod Maunder butcher with a display of Dartmoor meat

Our next visit was to Lloyd Maunder, the butcher in Bovey Tracey. This is the main retailer for the Association's produce, selling various cuts of beef and lamb straight from the moor. The deep red cuts of meat displayed in the window photographed very well.

Customers can also access Dartmoor Farmers' quality real beef and lamb by using their successful meat box delivery service. Produce can be supplied anywhere in the UK. Beyond the direct benefits to the farmers involved, the meat box scheme also serves to sustain the local tourism industry through the role traditional livestock farming has in maintaining the moorland landscape. Local hotels, pubs and restaurants are reliant on tourism generated by people's desire to enjoy Dartmoor's landscapes and natural offerings as they are, and without livestock farming it would look altogether different.

We were amazed by the outstanding flavour and taste of the prime rib of beef that was cooked for the recipe in this book. Clearly you can tell that great expertise had gone into producing such a wonderful piece of meat, it was absolutely delicious!!

We were also extremely impressed with the way in which the group has come together for the greater good. This is a wonderful co-operative model which is an inspiration to us all.

www.dartmoorfarmers.co.uk

Locally grown meat

Meat preparation

Dartmoor Farmers main outlet in Bovey Tracey

Dartmoor Farmers' prime rib of roasted beef with shallot and balsamic dressing

Peter Gorton

Ingredients – serves 6-8

1 x ask your butcher for a three rib roast, first cut, trimmed and tied
1 x tablespoon freshly ground pepper
2 x tablespoons of sea salt
2 x carrots, peeled
2 x onions diced roughly

Shallot and Balsamic Dressing

6 x large shallots
225ml x olive oil
3 x tablespoons balsamic vinegar
2 x tablespoons chopped fresh chives
Salt & pepper

Prime rib of beef roast makes an impressive dish for any occasion and for Christmas and other major holidays

Cooking the Beef

To ensure even cooking it is best to leave the beef rib joint at room temperature for about two hours.

Place oven rack on a lower level, heat oven to 455°F/gas 8/ 230°C/ fan oven 200°C
Rub beef with salt and pepper, seal meat in a frying pan until golden brown all over. Transfer to a heavy metal roasting pan. Arrange fat side up, place ribs on top of the onions and carrots. **Cook for twenty minutes.**

Reduce oven to 325°F/gas3/170°C/fan oven150°C

Continue cooking for one hour and twenty five minutes. Transfer to a meat platter and allow meat to rest for at least half an hour, this will allow all the juices to re-absorb and make it lovely and tender.

Shallot and Balsamic Dressing – Method
Prepare the vinaigrette - place the shallots and 175ml olive oil in a small ovenproof pan and cover tightly. **Bake at 350°F/180°F/ fan oven 160°F/gas 4 for one hour** or until the shallots are soft; let the shallots cool in the olive oil and then remove reserving the oil. Finally chop the shallots and put them in a bowl, add the balsamic vinegar and slowly whisk in the reserved olive oil. Add the chopped chives and season to taste with salt and pepper.

To Assemble
Slice beef and place on pre-heated dinner plates, spoon some roasted shallots and balsamic vinaigrette on top. Serve with vegetables and potato of your choice.

LANGAGE FARM

LANGAGE FARM IS mentioned in the Domesday book and has remained a working farmstead for over 900 years. However in 1980 the Harvey Family started to produce a range of 'Gold Top' from their Jersey herd to take full advantage of this fine raw material, rather send this into the liquid milk market which they felt rather devalued the product. 'Gold Top' was the early traditional brand of bottled 'Channel Island Milk' and was instantly recognised by the gold foil placed on the bottle's cap. This branding was to deliver the rich characteristics of the milk, being higher in butterfat and protein levels than the standard Friesian cow's milk. A firm favourite was to pour this over your cornflakes and watch as the golden creamy part of the milk covered your breakfast, Gosh! This takes me back to my youth when we used to fight for the top of the milk for our cereal!

The Harvey's found this was a way of adding value to the product which in turn allowed them to earn further income from the diversification which funded their children through university in a difficult financial climate. Thus they started to produce extra thick double and clotted cream and piloted this on family members and friends. Then word got round in the local community and the demand for the product grew, and continued to grow. This fuelled the Harvey's passion to produce a whole range of products and recipes to bring only the best products to the table. Today the company employs nearly fifty people with a herd of two hundred and eighty Jersey and Guernsey cows.

Langage produce over forty-five luscious ice cream, frozen yoghurts and sorbet flavours, and I think that on our visit there Adrian must have tried almost all of them by the look of his shirt when we finished filming for the day! Their other products include Langage clotted cream and double cream, crème fraiche, cream cheese and cottage cheese, and ice cream gateaux. All of these products can be tried at the superb Langage Farm shop in Plympton. One of the best things about this shop is its open seven days a week, so I know where Adrian will be on a Sunday!!

One warm summer's day we visited Langage to see what they do. Paul Winterton

The Langage ice cream van

Opposite: Contented Jerseys

warmly greeted us before leading us into a meeting room for a chat. Dan Ebsworth then took over and showed us around the plant and farm. The ice cream and clotted cream making process was fascinating. We looked around the factory and were walked through the production process with vats, freezers and mixers. In another room people packed and labelled clotted cream which was to be distributed around the country.

We went for a walk up to the original farm from where it all began. On the way back we wandered through the fields to see their happy herd of Jersey cows which do look stunning with their long eye lashes and their inquisitive natures.

Adrian agreed that they are definitely one of the more attractive breeds. For these are the real stars of Langage as you will see on the Langage website. A lot of the cows have names, like Hyacinth, Nora and Lulu just to mention a few, and a personal favourite of Peter's was Karen, the name appears on the 100ml & 500ml vanilla ice cream tubs. "Karen happens to be my wife's name," explains Peter.

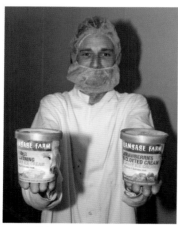

Irresistible!

Before we left, Adrian set up some product shots. As it was a nice day we took the photographs on the grass outside. The constant flow of ice cream that they brought out to photograph was melting in the sun so we had to work quickly. We couldn't let the ice cream go to waste! By the time we left we had eaten our own weight in about six flavours. It really is THAT good!

We must tell you about their modern clotted cream process; it has a traditional twist of separating the fat from the milk element of the cream. They then carefully test the milk solids content of the product in order to deliver constant butterfat to set the cream. The cream is then baked to their secret recipe to ensure the fats are caramelised to deliver that distinct nutty flavour and smooth texture to enjoy as part of the traditional Devonshire cream tea. When the cream baking is complete they carefully cool the cream to lock in the moisture and send the cream to their customers as soon as possible to ensure they receive a fresh quality cream.

Langage Farm today is run by the son James Harvey who has added a further innovation to ensure the business continues to push the boundaries. Langage is the first dairy company in the UK to have a farm manufacturing unit and an anaerobic digester on the same site. The anaerobic digester facility at the farm is an excellent working example of how localised closed-loop economy can be created.

Food waste that otherwise would have gone to landfill will instead be used to produce the energy that will power much of the production process on the farm. The food waste is processed and the gas produced by the food waste generates energy for the farm. The dried waste product is rich in nitrates so it is used on the fields to feed the grass that feeds the cows.

It will also allow Langage to educate the younger generation about the values of responsible recycling. The whole process is completely natural.

Langage have worked with over 400 Devon schools and have a passion to ensure younger people understand about farming, manufacturing and recycling. They invite youngsters to have fun and also to help in vital research as they have developed many bespoke ice-cream flavours with the students. They even have competitions between different schools producing and selling items such as ice cream gateaux for Christmas. These challenges ensure that children can learn vital skills, such as food technology, I.T. and design, presentation and communication, business economics, teamwork and above all the ability to enjoy themselves and revel in the unique experience.

On several occasions and with many different schools, these benefits have been mentioned in the school's OFSTED reports, and now the Langage Farm experience is being delivered in lessons locally as part of their curriculum. They have also extended this to foreign schools and often host French, Spanish and German students.

The staff really enjoy working with schools as they also get a chance to show off their skills, which is often very rewarding. Within the new anaerobic digester facility the company has now completed a purpose-built educational centre which is for all students of any age to enjoy!

All this allows them to produce the best possible award-winning dairy products on the market in a totally environmentally-friendly way. The many awards that Langage have won include the British Food Awards Gold Stars for their frozen yogurt, and at the Devon County Show the Champion Dairy producer two-years running, along with first prizes in class for clotted cream, soft cheese and numerous ice-cream flavours.

Paul Winterton the general manager summed up Langage for us by saying that "the products have been endorsed and enjoyed by many, and the growth of the business continues with the passion for excellence passed on through the workforce of over fifty local people , we now consider ourselves a centre of excellence in manufacture of dairy products, using Channel Island Milk and clean energy products. I can truly say we will constantly review the way we work and to continue to improve and bring to our customers the expertise they deserve. Our best is the least we can do."

Their best is very good indeed, as you could certainly tell by the smile and ice cream all over our faces when we left!

www.langagefarm.com

A healthy, wholesome and, above all, delicious range of products.

Langage Farm chocolate ice-cream with marinated oranges and lemon poppy seed shortbread
Peter Gorton

Ingredients – serves 6
1 x litre tub of Langage Farm
chocolate ice cream
6 x dessert rings or ramekin
moulds

Marinated Oranges
50g castor sugar
100ml water
150ml strained fresh
orange juice
½ vanilla pod seeds
scraped out and added
to the caramel
1 star anise
2 tablespoons grenadine
syrup
3 oranges segmented
Zest of 2 oranges

This is a very quick and easy dessert to produce but looks great for a special dinner

Method
Press the ice cream evenly into 6 x dessert rings and freeze for one hour.

Marinated Oranges – Method
Boil the castor sugar and water in a saucepan until the mixture turns into a caramel colour. Reduce the heat and add the orange juice and zest and cook for 5 minutes then add the grenadine syrup, vanilla pod seeds and star anise. Cook for another 5 minutes, finally pour over the segmented oranges in a bowl and allow to marinate for a day.

Lemon Poppy Seed Shortbread – Method
Pre-heat oven to 150°C/300°F/gas mark 2
Using a whisk beat the butter and sugar until creamy and smooth, about 2 minutes. Add the lemon juice, zest and vanilla and beat well.

In a bowl combine the flour, poppy seeds and salt, add the dry ingredients to the batter mixture and mix until well combined. Form the dough into a disk, wrap in plastic cling film and chill for at least 3 hours. Refrigerate for 3 days or freeze for two months.

Roll the dough between two sheets of greaseproof pepper to a ¼ inch thickness, place back in the refrigerator for ½ hour. Prick the shortbread with a fork and bake until pale golden all over 23-25 minutes. Remove from the oven a cut into a desired shape and cool on a wire rack.

To Serve
Take the ice cream out of the freezer and un-mould the ice cream. Place the ice cream on a shortbread biscuit; place another biscuit on top to make a sandwich. Arrange the marinated oranges around and serve immediately.

**Lemon Poppy Seed
Shortbread**
225g x softened unsalted
butter
150g x icing sugar
1½ teaspoon x fresh
lemon juice
1½ teaspoon x grated
lemon zest
½ teaspoon x vanilla extract
450g x flour sifted
1½ tablespoons x poppy seed
½ x teaspoon salt

Peter
Gorton

Sorting mussels on site by hand

EXMOUTH MUSSELS

IT'S 6.15AM in late July and the sun is already warm as we glide along between the yachts, watched by the usual three seals that live in the lower reaches of the River Exe in Devon. By 6.45am we already have the day's catch aboard, two and a half tons of gleaming black mussels teased from their muddy beds by the strangest boat I have ever seen, and we are heading back to 'headquarters', a 12-metre barge moored in the last bend of the river just before it meets the sea.

At the helm is Myles Blood Smyth who, with his wife Lisa, has built up an impressive mussel enterprise, farming their stock amongst all the yachts with hardly anyone being aware of what goes on beneath them. "It may look peaceful and serene on the surface," says Myles "but on the seabed there is an incredibly vibrant eco-system at work, an amazing ribbon of life winding left and right up the estuary, all based on the mussel beds that we have introduced."

Exmouth Mussels owner
Myles Blood Smyth

Myles appears happily obsessed with his mussels, showing me their growth rate and meat quality and telling me why this is one of the best rivers in England for shellfish. So how, I ask him, did it all start? "Fishing has been my passion for so long now that my previous life (a bit of pheasant farming and 12 years of thatching) is almost forgotten. Thatching was very rewarding but probably the loneliest job on the planet so I don't miss it one bit. Full time fishing meant less money and far more hardship – the best decision I ever made," he says, laughing.

"After a bit of trawling (boring) and several years potting for whelks (surprisingly interesting) I was diving in the Exe one day when I came across an enormous wild mussel bed. I had never seen anything quite as impressive as that before. The two main impacts on me were the sheer quantity of plants and animals dependent on the mussels for a living (they act like a marine version of trees in a rain forest) and the vast number of individuals involved, a number so large as to be beyond comprehension."

"I may be a bit sad but that was my 'road to Damascus' moment when I realised what this river had to offer and what absolutely marvellous chaps mussels were. You can have a blank area of sand one week and the next it can be covered in 1000 tons of jet black 2mm seed mussels which seem to appear from nowhere, providing you with a full year's work. All you have to do then is move them to a spot in the river where they are safe from storms and where the tidal flow will maximise their growth. During the following two years the river benefits enormously from the extra biomass and because they have been all kept together their own spawning is much more successful as well."

"Once they are big enough we start to harvest them but we do it relatively slowly so that all the dependent wildlife is able to move gradually over to the next bed along. By maintaining this high biomass there are huge benefits for all the other wildlife that thrives on the river, particularly the bird populations in winter which love the inter tidal beds that we provide. It is a truly symbiotic system, a way of earning a living by pure husbandry alone, adding nothing and damaging nothing in the process and we are all very proud of that."

Fishing in a Special Area of Conservation is a highly regulated and monitored business and so it should be, the Exe being one of the top wetland habitats in Europe. Most fishing processes are invasive but here at Exmouth Mussels they have come up with a cunning plan.

Dredges are banned in this river and their solution is a 'hovering-fluidiser' which uses water jets to peel the mussels off the bottom and send them up an elevator to the surface, washing them in the process. Over the following months the tide will gradually erode the rest of the mud that had built up under the mussels (which tend to trap the silt washed down during the winter storms) and the pristine, undamaged seabed will be revealed again, ready for the cycle to start once more.

The harvesting takes place on *Alibi*, a flat-topped French oyster barge that is covered in strange pipes and odd-looking machinery but which appears to be pretty clever stuff when you see it in action. "Not really," says Myles, "it's all common sense. The big pump and pipework are used to focus jets of water at the right angle on to the sea bed so we can roll the mussels up on to the elevator, and the rest is fairly simple."

"Mussels are quite sensitive and so it pays to be as gentle as possible. The benefit to us is that we can relay the same areas year after year, which is what I call intervening without interfering. This river provides us not only with a living but a way of life and she'll only do that if we are careful in the way we manage the special eco-systems here. In return we keep a look out for trouble and being on the river for 360 days a year means very little slips past us."

Heading out from Exmouth

Once the mature mussel has been washed and graded (all the small ones being returned along with any stray crabs) they are landed on to Exmouth Dock where they spend 42 hours in the purification tanks, getting rid of any grit and making sure they are safe to eat with ultra-violet light sterilising the water as they filter away happily in the natural way.

Next comes the polishing and hand-finishing process for which this farm is famous. "If I was a chef or someone cooking at home I would want a product that was ready to cook and that is what we aim for here," says Myles. "Natural mussels like ours, grown on the seabed, have much stronger shells than the rope-grown product and so we are able to clean them without losing shelf life which is a great bonus. I like to think that once someone has tried our mussels they won't want anyone else's ever again!'

Mussels are often sold packed in mesh bags but Myles has developed a 'protective atmosphere' packaging system which extends their shelf life up to seven days. "Putting our mussels into recycled trays and being able to seal in the moisture has been very successful for us. The packs are flushed with oxygen to keep the mussels happy and they have a much better chance of getting to the customer in top shape," says Myles. "This has proved very popular with food businesses who appreciate that smaller packs designed around the portions needed for the restaurant trade helps to reduce wastage."

Fresh, healthy mussels

The final part of the story is, where does it all go? How do you sell three tonnes of mussels every week? "About half goes up to London to some of the smartest restaurants in the land," says Myles, "but the rest is sold locally, the demand gradually increasing year by year which is great. I love wandering into one of the gastro-pubs around here and seeing people tucking into a big bowl of mussels and it's especially nice to see kids giving it a try. Some years we have too much full-size stock for ourselves and then we export the extra to Yerseke in Holland, so we're even helping with the budget deficit as well!"

We accompanied Myles out into the Estuary and met up with the rest of the crew. We watched the process that Myles has explained so well, from the careful dredging for the mussels to washing and sorting. All completed on a barge out in the estuary. Watching Myles and his team at work you are struck by several thoughts. This is obviously a serious commercial operation and the production pace is very impressive. Staffing levels are high when you do this type of work and it is easy to see the boys are well motivated and highly trained. With nine people in full time employment this small innovative company is making a significant contribution to the local economy.

Normally with industry on this scale comes environmental compromise but in this case there does not seem to be a down side. Once the beds of tiny seed mussels are 're-housed'

in quiet areas of the river, nature takes over again and does the rest. This now stable bio-mass provides habitat niches and feeding opportunities for everything in the food chain, right up to the birds and finally to man himself. It all harks back to the old days when man and nature were in balance and it's heartening to find such a good news fishing story here in the Devon countryside.

When we cooked the mussels at Peter's restaurant for the book recipe we were treated some of the best shellfish we have ever eaten.

www.exmouthmussels.com

Oriental Style Mussels

Peter Gorton

Ingredients
1kg x fresh live Exmouth Mussels
15g x butter
1 x stick lemon grass/crushed (optional)
10g x chopped shallots
100ml x white wine
10g x chopped garlic
Juice of x 1 lime
10g x fresh chilli
6 x large tomatoes, skinned & diced
400ml tin coconut milk
10g x chopped ginger
20ml x olive oil
Chopped coriander – to taste
Chopped basil – to taste

Method

Wash, clean and de-beard the mussels, discarding any that stay open. Sauté the shallots, garlic, ginger and chilli in the olive oil. Add the crushed lemon grass and mussels to the pan and pour in the white wine, place a lid on the pan and cook and shake the pan until all the mussels have opened.

Add the tin of coconut milk and cook for one minute to heat through, add the tomatoes, lime juice and chopped coriander and basil. Finally pour into a serving dish with fresh crusty bread on the side.

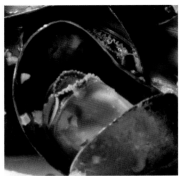

NORSWORTHY DAIRY GOATS

HIGH UP ON A HILL above Crediton sits Frankland Cottage at Gunstone. Through the gate and I am greeted by dozens of goats of all sizes, in the barns, the fields and in outdoor pens. They certainly have plenty of character and are very noisy. Amongst the various outbuildings sits a newer unit. This is where the magic happens. A purpose-built cheese making facility.

Norsworthy Dairy Goats was established in 1999 with 40 kids. They then looked for someone who would take the milk. For cow farmers there are various businesses that will take the milk, but for goat's milk its not easy. They eventually found Ticklemore Cheese, based in Totnes, who already had a goat milk supply but said they could do with more milk throughout the months from August until March. The milking parlour was then bought in second hand and the bulk tank was fitted. A year later they were producing milk that was sold to specialist cheese and yoghurt makers. Dave Johnson runs the business with his wife Marilyn supplying outlets in the Devon area. When Ticklemore no longer wanted the milk they decided to freeze it. The following year they used the frozen milk to feed the young kids. Then they were hit by the Foot and Mouth outbreak. For six months no milk was sold. They froze all the milk and had 5000 litres in freezers in Exeter. This milk couldn't be used for cheese but could be used to feed the kids.

Below and opposite:
Dave and Marilyn Johnson

Once the Foot and Mouth outbreak subsided Dave went back to relief milking while Marilyn was miking the herd at home. They had all this milk that Ticklemore couldn't take, so what could they do with it?

They found a lady in North Devon, Vera, who could make the cheese, so the milk was taken up to her. She would make the cheese and Dave would bring it back down to mature it. Then followed farmers markets at which the cheese sold well. The Vera retired so a new plan was formulated. Planning permission was gained for the dairy in 2005 and they got a grant towards building it.

In September 2006 the dairy was making cheese, still with Vera's help, but with Dave learning from Vera and starting to make cheese himself.

Today there are three different types of hard and medium soft cheese made: Norsworthy, Gunstone and Posbury, along with soft cheeses, Chelwood (a fresh curd cheese, plain or with herbs) Chelwood Ash ,Tillerton (a mould-ripened brie style log) and Nanny Bloo. This last is a blue cheese which leaves a tingle on your tongue. It is made off the premises to avoid cross-contamination by the blue spores. The Chelwood Ash is a fresh cheese with a striking appearance and distinctive taste and texture. This comes in the shape of a log and is rolled in edible charcoal.

Norsworthy Dairy Goats now have around 170 goats comprising the Saanen, Alpine and Toggenburg breeds. Using a cattle comparison Marilyn says, the Saanen is comparable to the Friesian cow, the Alpine is like an Ayrshire and the Toggenburg is similar to the Channel Island breeds. "We don't breed for yield, we breed for solids as we want the highest level of cheese from every litre of milk," she tells us.

"We don't milk yield record and the goats don't kid every year as their level lactations will persist for two to three years whilst they are producing for cheese. The main time you lose a goat is at kidding so if you don't need to why put them through the stress," says Dave.

Feeding is watched with care. Whatever they eat comes straight through to the milk. Everything they eat is brought on to the farm. Their diet is based on ad-lib hay placed high up in the feeders to encourage natural behaviour, and also includes brewers grains. Marilyn admits there is very little knowledge about goat nutrition so they have had to find it out for themselves.

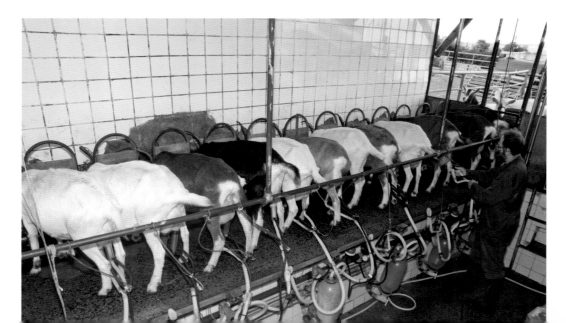

"Eventually," says David, "we will scale up the production with a larger herd to increase milk production. The goats produce about 4-5 litres of milk for about 2 years before they go back for breeding to produce the next generation."

The cheese

The milk goes from the bulk tank that's filled from the milking parlour into the cheese vat. The milk is then heated to about 30 degrees. Then the rennet is added and then the milk starts to set. The vat holds about 1200 litres of milk from a milking herd of 170 goats. Once it has started to set then the curd is cut by the motorised blades set into the vat into one inch chunks. The solids are the curds and the cloudy liquid is the whey. This isn't used and is irrigated on to the farm land.

Once the curd has rested the whey is drained off from the bottom of the vat. The cheese is then stirred and hot water is added to raise the cheese temperature. The blades are reversed in the vat to the non sharpened sides to stir the cheese rather than chop it.

The cheese is then scooped out and packed into plastic moulds with nets inside. A lid is then placed into the container ready for pressing. The soft curd sits in nets and is not pressed. The first cheese taken out is the plain Norsworthy and then herbs are added for the Posbury. Once the cheese is packed into the containers weights are applied to the tops to squeeze out the fluids and harden the cheese.

Long log shape cheeses were laid out on greaseproof paper ready to be wrapped and labelled by Marilyn. They make cheese two to three times a week from their growing herd.

Marilyn with a young kid

Together in the barn

101

Feeding time at Norsworthy

Later in the day I visited the milking parlour for the daily ritual. A very similar set up to milking cows but scaled down in size. The goats are very entertaining to watch and there is a definitely a hierarchy with certain goats having a certain spot to stand. I was amazed by how much character they had.

Afterwards I accompanied Marilyn out in the fields with a hundred or so goats all after the bucket of feed she was carrying and I trod in a few unmentionables whilst concentrating on photographing the goats. We also met a few kids in the barns, each with huge ears and big smiles! Real characters. I can see why many people keep goats.

Norsworthy Dairy Goats also sell goat's milk and make yoghurt. Dave and Marilyn attend many Farmers markets and shows to promote and sell their wonderful products.

So to what do they owe their remarkable success? Dave says he would put it down to clean milk, general hygiene and the fact that they make it so quickly after milking. The milk travels less than ten yards from the goat to the cheese vat. The milk does not wait around long and it doesn't have time to get that 'goaty taint' so the cheese has a nice mild clean and fresh flavour.

Peter produced a fantastic Norsworthy goat's cheese parcel for the book recipe. I was fortunate enough to try it and I recommend you do too.

www.norsworthydairygoats.blogspot.com

Out in the fields

Goats Milk facts

• Sales of goat's milk products have increased by 20% year on year for much of the past decade. Yet small producers find it hard to market and promote the products due to the lack of an infrastructure.

• Nutritionally goat's and cow's milk is fairly similar, but in goat's milk the fat globules are one fifth of the size of those in cow's milk. (It is said to be naturally homogenised)

• Goat's milk is said to be more easily digested.

• Goat's milk can often replace cow's milk in the diets of those with allergies.

• Goat's milk and butter is white because goats produce milk with yellow beta-carotene converted to a colourless form of vitamin A.

Norsworthy baked goat's cheese in Indian pastry with sweet & sour leeks

Peter Gorton

Ingredients - Serves 4
Indian Pastry
225g x plain flour
1 x egg
2 x tablespoons olive oil
1 x teaspoon curry powder
Pinch of salt
100ml x yoghurt
1 x tablespoon water
1 x teaspoon cumin

Goat's cheese in Indian pastry
55g x roughly chopped hazelnuts, chestnuts & pistachios
175g x Norsworthy goat's cheese
55g x butter

Sweet and Sour Leeks
2 x large leeks
1x tablespoon sugar
Juice of 1 x lemon
2 x cloves of garlic
4 x tablespoons olive oil
1 x tablespoon soy sauce (optional)

The leeks and Indian pastry with Norsworthy goat's cheese are a perfect combination, you won't stop eating these!

Indian Pastry – Method
In a mixing bowl combine the flours with the spice mix, cumin and curry powder. Make a well in the middle and add the salt, egg, yoghurt, oil and water and mix to a smooth dough. Knead for 5 minutes & then allow to rest for 30 minutes. If the pastry feels a little wet just add some more flour.

Chef's Tip
Indian Pastry is very versatile and can be pan-fried lightly or baked in the oven.

Goat's cheese in Indian pastry – Method
Pre-heat oven to 200°C/fan oven 180°C/gas 6
Cut the goat's cheese into the desired shape for wrapping in the pastry and place on a flat surface and brush with butter and sprinkle over the chopped nuts and then set aside. Roll out the Indian pastry and cut four round circles large enough for the cheese and shape the pastry around the cheese and tuck the ends underneath. Repeat with the others. Place in the fridge to firm for five minutes.

Heat up a frying pan with a little oil and cook the goat's cheese parcels until golden brown, be careful they do not burn. Place on an oven tray and set aside. (These parcels can also be deep-fried until golden brown and puffed up)

Sweet and Sour Leeks – Method
Clean the leeks thoroughly. Cut off the tough green part. Cut the leeks into longish slices.

Fry the crushed garlic and sugar in hot oil until the sugar caramelises slightly. Add the leeks and turn them a little over moderate heat. Sprinkle with lemon juice. Cover and stew gently over a low heat until tender. Serve hot or cold.

To Assemble
Return the goat's cheese to the oven for four minutes or until hot. Place a small mound of the leeks in the middle of each plate and place a goat's cheese parcel on top. This dish will be good with a tomato dressing or red pepper and basil.

Chef's Tip
You can use a pasta machine to roll out the pastry very thin just like pasta lasagne sheets if you like.

HERON VALLEY ORGANIC JUICES

HERON VALLEY ORGANIC JUICES list their address as 'Crannacombe Farm, Deepest Devon' and on arrival, driving down what seemed like an endless narrow lane, it certainly felt like it! The farm, where the business is based, is set in beautiful South Devon countryside, with orchards resting on the rolling hills in Loddiswell near Kingsbridge.

History

Natasha grew up on the family farm, which has been owned by her parents since the 1970s. They bought the place virtually derelict, restored it and then started producing fruit juice and cider. Natasha grew up with the fruit juices and cider, helping at shows and enjoying the whole thing. She left home at the age of 22 to travel around Europe, working in the surf industry and even running a specialist bike shop in Dorset. Circumstances changed and she became disillusioned with the commercial world she was involved in and she eventually returned to the farm with two young children. Strong links to the valley strengthened her desire to return home. Her parents were still running the apple and cider business on the farm and were thinking of retiring. The juices were still being produced in the farm buildings and an old scout hut was used as the labelling shed. Very much still a cottage industry. But the business was growing so Natasha approached her parents with a plan and took over the juice business in 2006. Natasha lives on the farm near the main house in a restored cottage with her husband and three children Jasmin, Cosmo and Oliver.

After taking over Heron Valley Juices, a large wooden farm building was constructed to allow the business to meet the greater demand. Natasha, a delightful, energetic character says she is an optimist which definitely helps as she admits to making just about every mistake there is whilst cutting her teeth. She speaks fondly of her parents every time she mentions her Mum and Dad and admits they were a great help during the early days. Lessons were learned and things improved every year to the point that her eyes can now be firmly fixed on the part of the business she loves – the juice.

Opposite: The Heron Valley team

Top: The press
Above: Unloading after sterilising

Opposite, clockwise from top left: Cider barrels; sorting the fruit; loading the press; pressing with acacia boards; labels; bottling by hand

Natasha is obviously passionate about the product. She loves food and the honesty of the way their juices are produced. Over the last few years she has gradually expanded the business to three and a half times where it was when she started, supplying numerous Devon retailers and larger outlets, like Darts Farm, near Exeter.

The production methods are all about the taste and what is in the juice. The fruit is hand selected and picked. They have a great relationship with all their suppliers which range from a few pallets of apples to many tons. Natasha stressed that she likes knowing where all her fruit is coming from and the people behind it.

A hands-on approach to the selection, pressing and blending allows her to keep the standards very high, backed up by a very efficient team that she describes as family like environment.

Natasha believes an important role is to communicate with the people she meets and promote the many virtues of her product and the differences to the 'carton on a supermarket shelf'.

Natasha appeared from a well-used Land Rover and warmly greeted me. She immediately struck me as a friendly, likeable and very optimistic lady. We sat on some pallets outside and chatted about Heron Valley. She is obviously passionate about what she does.

Natasha introduced me to her friendly and enthusiastic team. A good relationship with your team and no 'them and us' feeling makes all the difference. Coming from a supermarket background myself I understand the sentiment exactly.

The 'team' were busy filling and labelling bottles and pressing apples. The mostly female team, includes her older sister, Britta.

The Product

To produce the juice and keep up with demand Heron Valley needs more and more reliable sources of eating apples, they are certified organic so need organically grown fruit. This is why Heron Valley is looking at planting additional orchards as a number of those they currently use have become elderly as have the owners! Many of the orchards are biennial so you have a great year followed by a poor year for yield. Once they have the crops a pressing plan is organised. Most eating apples are great for juice, Natasha avoids Russett apples as they leave sediment in the juice.

All the fruit is washed and hand graded. Fruit that doesn't make the grade is fed to neighbours 'very happy' pigs or the family's herd of South Devon Cattle. The fruit is then

fed through the milling machine, diced and ends up as a pommace. This process breaks up the fibres and releases the juice. About 1.3kg of fruit goes into each bottle. No additives (other than vitamin C) or water are used at all.

The pressing is made of layers of 'cheeses'– these are cloths into which four scoops of pommace are added, folded over and then covered with an acacia board. These are built up in layers. The four scoops is important . Too much pommace in a cheese risks an 'apple explosion' resulting in the press operator and immediate area getting an apple coating. The hydraulic press squeezes the juice out and into a tank below.

The juice is then pumped into a header tank ready for the next part of its journey which leads to a hand-fed gravity bottling process. Here the bottles are hand filled and capped. The juice is an entirely natural product with no preservatives, so it is then pasturised by placing the bottles in water tanks that are temperature controlled to 72 degrees for half an hour. This kills all the bacteria in the juice so it will then keep. This is why it is important to carefully check the quality of the fruit at the selection stage.

The bottles then move on to the fantastic new 'Wallace & Gromit' labelling machine that prints the dates on the labels and sticks them on to the bottles.

Opposite, The juice press

Ready for sale

113

Future

Natasha is now thinking 'what do we want to do?' and after much deliberation has decided that she is happy how she is, 'small and beautifully formed'. Being a larger outfit brings compromises. Heron Valley is all about quality, hands on and personally produced with care using a natural local product. "We make a nice living and enjoy what we do."

Her next project is to restore and plant new orchards in her locality. A long-term plan is to buy the buildings from her parents and utilise the fifteen acres around them for apples. Then to re-establish traditional and bush orchards for juices and cider production. The sloping valleys around them are perfect for apple trees.

The juice is about 80% of the business with the cider at 20%. Natasha is also keen to increase the cider production and enjoys the 'wonderful alchemy' of it.

"There are easier ways of making money and it's hard work, but the satisfaction that comes with it all is worth it," Natasha says. A thought which is echoed by many of the other 'Food Heroes' in this book.

"Nothing makes me happier than being at a show and handing a sample of juice to someone and knowing exactly what's in it, how it was made and where it came from."

"I know that they will love it."

A good relationship with the stockists is also important and the sales are up on year on year which is excellent in the current climate.

Natasha is also investing soon in a newer apple press. The existing one which is about 30 years old she bought off her parents, and it was second hand when they bought it. Many tons of apples have passed through it over the years.

"Due to the whole production process being by hand the efficiency of the press is important as the business thrives, especially at this time of year (September) when the apples are in abundance," says Natasha.

Heron Valley

Every year something goes wrong with it but she plans to keep the original press as part of the story.

Heron Valley also invite schools in for visits to show the children how the business runs and that anybody can become an 'apple geek' as Natasha affectionately puts it.

The company are also 'organic'. This is a difficult 'label' to keep as the certification process and rigours of the process are quite challenging. "I am more inclined towards producing a great product in a sustainable way than being solely focused on its organic status — origin, care of the environment and the quality of ingredients are all paramount."

Over the years Natasha said she had been offered some strange products that were described as 'organic'. One example was an organic ginger extract for flavouring to improve the taste. Natasha's response was what is wrong with using real stem ginger?. How will this improve the product, and is it actually ginger?

It turned out it wasn't ginger, but the gene from a strawberry mixed with the gene from mint which gives a ginger taste! That struck Natasha as being an horrific, Frankenstein approach. All the salesman could say was "but it will be cheaper"!

Needless to say the salesman went away without a sale. Natasha firmly wants her juice to be as far away from this approach as physically possible.

All in all Heron Valley is a fantastic food producer with real heart and with great sustainable ideas that I am sure will thrive as the years pass.

www.heronvalley.co.uk

Natasha

Pan-fried scallops and John Dory on a wild rice pancake with Heron Valley Cider

Peter Gorton

Ingredients – serves x 4

4 x John Dory fillets
8 x scallops

Wild rice and cider pancakes – Makes about 15 pancakes

1 x tablespoon chopped spring onions
2 x small apples peeled and diced small
1 x egg
1 x egg yolk
200ml x milk
100ml cider
350g x cooked wild rice
2 x teaspoon peanut oil/vegetable oil
1 x teaspoon butter
1 x teaspoon of cumin, saffron etc. optional
225g x plain flour
1 x tablespoon baking powder
Oil for cooking
1 x tablespoon of fresh herbs, optional

Method

Heat an oven proof pan large enough to hold the fish fillets in one layer. Add the two tablespoons of olive oil and when it is hot lay the fillets in the pan and sear on one side for one minute, transfer and put under a hot grill to finish cooking, about three minutes. The fillets do not need to be flipped. Set aside and keep warm.

Cooking scallops

Sear the scallops in a hot pan with a tablespoon of oil, place scallops in and cook until golden brown, about 1 minute, flip scallops over and brown, take out and let rest and keep warm.

Wild rice and cider pancakes – Makes about 15 pancakes

Sauté the spring onions and apples in olive oil for 2 minutes, place the egg, egg yolk and milk and cider in a medium bowl and whisk until well blended. Sift together the flour and baking powder and add to the egg mixture and whisk until smooth. Fold in the wild rice, herbs etc. Set aside.

Heat up a small frying pan and shallow fry in oil on one side until golden brown then flip and brown the other side, using a pastry cutter cut out to the required size and place in the centre of a warmed plate. Place a fillet of John dory on top of the pancake and place the scallops around, serve with a sauce of your choice.

Chefs tip
These wild rice pancakes also go with meat like pork, duck and pigeon. I use Heron Valley cider to make wonderful gravy for one of the pork dishes I cook at Gorton's restaurant.

OTTERTON MILL

Introduction

I AM SITTING WITH Simon Spiller having a coffee, and he was telling Adrian and me about Otterton Mill. He said "You can see the cows in the field and go in the farm shop and buy the beef and milk, but we are the equivalent in terms of bread, flour and cakes and baked goods. As far as I know, we are the only place in Devon and perhaps the South West where you can come and see the flour ground and the bread baked and walk away with the goods."

Prior to taking on Otterton Mill, Simon and his wife Caroline had no background in catering or food. Simon was a management consultant and Caroline was in marketing for airlines. They were living in the city and when their daughter was five they decided they wanted a lifestyle change to be able to see more of each other. Simon used to travel a lot, so they decided to move back to Devon where they had grown up. They said they didn't realise what it takes to run a seven day catering and visitor attraction.

Not only is there a working watermill and bakery, the Mill is also home to an award-winning café-restaurant, a craft and gift shop, a very nice gallery and a highly regarded acoustic music venue for a range of genres from folk to blues, jazz to Americana. There's a lovely outdoor setting for about one hundred people in the summer, with a little stage covered by a pergola, whilst, in the winter, the gigs are hosted inside in the intimate restaurant setting in a room for about fifty people. Artists from all over the world come because of the Mill's reputation. Caroline runs this venue and is approached by ten to fifteen artists a week asking for a booking.

As you enter the courtyard, you'll be met by the aroma of freshly baked bread. Using age-old techniques and only natural ingredients, they bake a signature range of wholemeal (using their own stone ground flour), strong white, granary, spelt and rye breads, plus the speciality pan gallegos and speckled hen breads.

The mill leat

History of Mill

There has been a working mill at Otterton since at least Norman times, when William the Conqueror granted all the local land hereabouts to the abbots of St Michel of Normandy. The earliest written record of the mill is in the Domesday survey in 1068, which confirmed its status as one of the largest and most productive of the seventy mills in Devon. At this time, there was sufficient water power for the mill to be using three sets of mill-stones. Otterton Manor estate (and its mill) remained under French rule for 400 years until Henry V took it back and gave it to the nuns of Syon Abbey. Later, when Henry VIII ordered the dissolution of the monasteries, the manor was sold to Richard Duke and remained with his family for 200 years. In 1785, the estate was sold to Denys Rolle, whose family was subsequently joined in marriage with the Clinton family. To this day, the mill and much of the surrounding land remains part of the Clinton Devon Estate.

Many millers have worked the mill over the years, but one who left his mark is John Uglow, who milled at Otterton from 1843 to 1864, with a rent of £100 a year. He was also

3. The rate of feeding the grain into the mill stones, as set by raising or lowering the shaker shoe under the hopper. The slower the feed the finer the flour. If the grain stops flowing for any reason, the mill stones will grind against each other, get overheated, worn and probably damaged.

Dressing the Stones: Every 100 to 200 tonnes of grain, the mill stones have to be dressed. In use, the faces of the stones become polished and the grooves for pulling in the grain become too shallow. Dressing involves roughening the surfaces of the mill stones and re-cutting the grooves. Dressing the stones is a highly skilled job as the working surfaces of the stones have to remain perfectly flat.

Otterton Mill are remarkably fortunate to have three wonderful men as their millers, Brian Hart, Jerry Tottle and Graham Richardson. All three are volunteers and bring a wealth of experience, skill and enthusiasm to what they do. "Not only do they mill the stone-ground flour for which we are famous, but they also look after the ancient mill machinery and preserve it in full working order," Simon tells us. The fourth member of the team is Graham Smith, or 'young' Graham as he is affectionately known. Graham represents the next generation of millers at Otterton, and is currently learning the ancient skills of milling from his colleagues.

The primary grain used is organic Maris Widgeon wheat, which is specially grown for them by Tamarisk Farm on the Devon and Dorset border. Maris Widgeon is one of the oldest and tallest varieties of wheat, and is increasingly rare, but it makes the best wholemeal bread. Roy, the Head Baker, insists on it! Milling usually takes place twice a month and produces about 12 tonnes of flour throughout the year. If you visit on one of their milling days you can watch the millers at work and taste the flour as it arrives fresh and warm from the mill stones.

The bakery

Otterton Mill also produces mouth-watering cakes, shortbreads, slices and their famous scones. Unlike other bakeries, the Mill is open seven days a week, so you can enjoy the bread every day, baked freshly each morning. The cheese scones are fantastic too, made from a recipe which is a closely guarded secret.

Adrian visited the bakery early one morning to watch Roy the baker perform his magic. He watched in awe as waves of fantastic bread, cakes and scones flowed forth from the oven, and he reminisced with Roy as he once was a baker himself!

Future

Simon and Caroline love what they do and want to continue the legacy of celebrating local foods and arts, ancient traditions, and world class music. The Mill today is a showcase for some of the best food and art of the South West. Being in a tourist area, half their trade is crammed into five months in the summer. In the winter, there is a full programme of classes and workshops covering crafts, bakery courses and photography classes which Adrian runs all of which fill up very quickly. A planning application has been put in to build a classroom to offer more room and hands-on experience. And we haven't yet mentioned the bushcraft area just outside in the car park. It is full of wildlife, otters, kingfishers and a pond with trout and eels. The main purpose of the area is to run bush courses, and to provide a quiet retreat. The Mill also houses a wildlife shop, alongside homeware and cookware, and has a busy special events calendar running throughout the year. To sum up Otterton Mill, Simon said "It's a fantastic gathering place to enjoy great food, a warm Devon welcome, beautiful countryside and to explore and enjoy all the Mill has to offer." We entirely agree!

www.ottertonmill.com

Peter Gorton's Brown Bread Rolls

Ingredients

140g x Otterton Mill wholemeal flour
95g x strong white flour
15g x butter
125ml x water/milk
20g x yeast

Method

Pre-heat oven 200°C

In a mixer combine the flours and salt. In a pan mix the milk and water and heat to around 37°c (tepid/no hotter). Mix in the yeast and stir until dissolved, now add the melted butter and carefully add this in stages into the mixed flours and mixing all the time.

Once it all has combined continue to mix until it becomes a smooth dough and pulls away easily from the sides of the mixing bowl, it should feel a little bit sticky, take the mixing bowl with the bread in it and cover with a damp cloth and leave in a warm area of your kitchen, until the dough has doubled in bulk.

Cut the dough into small pieces, each weighing about 60g, with your clenched fist press down on each piece several times to expel the air.

Shaping the dough – to shape each piece of dough, cup the palm of the hand over it and rotate your hand continuously until the dough gathers up into a round ball. Repeat. Cover the rolls with a damp cloth and leave them to rise for about twenty five minutes until doubled in bulk.

Baking the rolls

Pre-heat oven to 450°f/gas 8/230°c/fan oven 210°c

To give the finished rolls a hard lightly seasoned crust; brush them with salted water just before putting in the oven. Bake the rolls for about fifteen to twenty five minutes until browned. Transfer the rolls to a wire rack to cool before serving.

Show tunnel

before adding. Some such as Ancho and Mulato chillies have quite thick skins so may need pushing through a sieve to take the bits out first.

There is usually no reason why dried chillies can't be powdered instead of soaking. The main advantage of storing them dried whole rather than as powder is that powder will quickly lose the aromas and flavours. There is nothing to stop you grinding them in a coffee grinder and using the powder.

You can dry your own chillies by hanging them either in the sun if the air is dry or in an airing cupboard. For something more serious try a foil-lined box with a light bulb in it, which should do the trick in a day or two.

Spelling

'Chilli' or 'Chile' - The choice is yours. 'Chile' is the more usual spelling in the USA, and 'chilli' is generally accepted as the correct UK spelling. You may also see 'chili' which is also used in the USA. We have decided to use the UK spelling since that is where we are, but you may use whichever you prefer.

Sowing Seeds

In the UK chilli seeds need to be sown early in the year, and grown on in a greenhouse or poly-tunnel though they can be grown outside in a sunny spot during the height of summer. Germination can be very variable between varieties and can take as much as five weeks, though the varieties the Chilli Farm sell on their seed page should all germinate within 10-14 days. To help you get going, they have listed some of the tricks and guidelines they use to give their chillies the best start possible and for growing them on in pots.

The Chilli Farm, shop and cafe are open for visitors all year. They can wander among the fruiting chilli plants, sample all of the sauces, preserves and chocolate made on the farm and in the growing season take away fresh chillies, chilli seedlings, plants and seeds.

Chilli Chocolate

There are the six delicious flavours of chilli chocolate, including an extreme version, all made on the farm - Original, Orange, Peppermint, Fruit and Spice and Coffee-Bean. All five flavours contain a unique blend of chillies.

Warning: you may find the chilli chocolate a little hotter than other brands you have tried - nothing outrageous, but certainly warm enough to notice! The chilli chocolate is now also available as a drink – just add warm milk!

Peter was excited about the chocolate as it brought back memories of when he appeared on 'Little Chefs' on local TV and the recipe was chilli chocolate brownie using their chocolate. They won the episode with the recipe.

Latest

Jason and Steve were very pleased to recently announce the official opening of the new building on the farm: "The view from the new café is wonderful. Our customers have been saying what a difference the new shop and café have made," said Steve.

The new building took 12 months to complete and has resulted in a bright, airy and welcoming space for eating, drinking and shopping. The shop shelves are filled with chilli preserves, sauces and chocolates, made on-site with chillies grown on the farm.

Customers visiting the farm can enjoy tasters of all the South Devon Chilli Farm range of products and wander through the chilli display area featuring over 100 varieties of chilli plants. The farm is free to visit and is open all year.

The new café has an array of chilli-themed dishes as well as traditional Devon café options such as cakes, cream teas, pasties and jacket potatoes. For chilli fans, the menu includes Mexican dishes such as burritos, quesadillas and an ever-changing list of spicy specials. The café is available for special events and there are plans to add evening opening in the near future.

The growth of the South Devon Chilli Farm has been well documented in the media with numerous features in national newspapers as well as TV appearances on BBC Gardeners World, BBC Country File, ITV, West Country TV and UKTV Food. They are also recommended by Jamie Oliver who says, "As you know I am a Chilli freak and these guys grow the best in the country." Tom Parker-Bowles, food writer and confirmed chilli lover has also recommended their products in his regular *Sunday Mail* column.

You may also see South Devon Chilli Farm products for sale in farm shops and delicatessens near you. They supply many local outlets in the West Country and have extended distribution to other shops nationwide

www.southdevonchillifarm.co.uk